P9-BJW-406

PINOT

Gamay

Gewurztraminer

Fleurie

ORVIETO

PIESPORTER

For José,

Companion at
many a tasting of
odd wines.

Alex

August 1973

Also by Alexis Bespaloff

THE SIGNET BOOK OF WINE

ALEXIS BESPALOFF'S

Guide to
Inexpensive Wines

Illustrated by Paul Bacon

SIMON AND SCHUSTER : NEW YORK

SBN 671-21502-7
Library of Congress Catalog Card Number: 72-93505
Designed by Irving Perkins
Manufactured in the United States of America
Printed by Mahony & Roese, Inc., New York, N.Y.
Bound by H. Wolff Book Mfg. Co., Inc., New York, N.Y.

1   2   3   4   5   6   7   8   9   10

Contents

Introduction, 9

Wine drinking is more subjective than horse racing and nearly as subjective as love, but the gamble is less; you get something for your money no matter what you pick.

—A. J. Liebling

It is the mark of an intelligent person to look for precision in all things only so far as the nature of the subject permits.

—Aristotle

Introduction

This guide is a personal selection—with commentary—of nearly 350 inexpensive wines from all over the world that are generally available throughout the United States.

My working price limit was $3.50 but more than half the selections cost less than $2.50. In addition, a number of wines that cost $3.50 to $4.50 are included in the listings from such well-known wine regions as Beaujolais, Bordeaux, Burgundy, and the Rhine and Moselle. Not all of these selections represent the best wine values, but they are dependable examples of wines that are becoming expensive. They can be used to judge the quality and comparative value of less expensive brands that may be available locally, such as wines with limited distribution and wines specially labeled for individual retailers, none of which are included in this guide.

I have been tasting wines professionally for almost ten years, and my notebooks contain comments on about 10,000 wines tasted in barrel and in bottle. Nevertheless, when I began this book I decided to ignore my previous tasting notes and to base my recommendations entirely on wines currently available in this country. My selections were made from more than 2,000 wines that I tasted specifically for this book, many of them two or three times. With the exception of 60 or 70 bottles that friends in the wine trade sent along to me, I bought all of these wines in retail liquor stores. It may seem presumptuous to base a book entirely on my own preferences, but I think it would be even more presumptuous to write about specific wines without tasting them, much less recommend them to others. Moreover, my experience suggests that most wine drinkers have no trouble picking out the best wines at a tasting, as long as they react to the wine, rather than to its label. I have simply opened up a great many bottles in an attempt to find those that offer the best value. The tastings themselves were almost all blind, that is, the bottles were covered and the glasses numbered. Blind tastings are the only way to judge the quality of popular wines irrespective of their reputation, or to discover good values among unfamiliar wines.

One way to use this book is to work from the representative selection of 120 inexpensive wines on page 139. These lists are meant to demonstrate the wide range of wines available for under $3.50 and I hope my recommendations include wines that are new to you at a price you want to pay. There are, of course, several very successful brands that are still among the best values, just as there are a number of popular wines that seem to me overpriced. Conversely, just because a wine is unusual or little known does not necessarily make it worth seeking out; it may be unknown for good reason. Appendix 2 lists 50 wines available in gallons and half-gallons, including some of the least expensive wines in general distribution.

Appendix 3, Comparative Price Ranges of Inexpensive Wines, also constitutes a complete list of the individual sections that make up this book. It is impossible to talk about wine without talking about where it comes from, but although these sections are arranged by country and district of origin, I have tried to focus on individual appellations, that is, on the names with which wines are actually labeled. These appellations, which do not always coincide with a wine's geographical origin, are shown in **boldface**. The most important appellations are listed at the head of each section; others are sometimes mentioned in the descriptive text.

If a number of popular appellations are described at greater length than their comparative value merits, it is because I have tried to suggest the most sensible approach to buying such readily available wines. Conversely, several unfamiliar wines that are inexpensive and in abundant supply are only described briefly because there is not much useful to say about them except to recommend them to your attention.

Everyone must determine for himself the combination of quality and price that determines value. Any wine that sells for $4 a gallon—the equivalent of 80 cents a bottle—is considered excellent value by some people, as long as it can be swallowed without harm. Others will insist that no wine that costs less than, say, $2.50 can really be good. One factor that determines how much you have to pay for a wine is how distinctive it is. Wines such as Beaujolais, red Burgundy, Gewürztraminer, Rhine and Moselle, and California Zinfandel have such an individual taste that if you buy poor examples you will lose precisely the personality that makes these wines interesting. There are other wines, such as Pommard, Châteauneuf-du-Pape, Valpolicella and Soave, Chablis and Pouilly-

Fuissé, that are so popular that their price is determined as much by fame and scarcity as by the quality of the wine itself. Buying cheap examples of these wines is not the solution, however—by paying too little for a high-priced wine you often pay too much for the wine that is actually in the bottle. A better solution is to turn to the many less familiar but soundly made wines of the world that are in abundant supply and still attractively priced.

There are certain red wines whose best examples are not cheap but whose inexpensive examples are not bad value. A Chianti or *petit château* from Bordeaux at $2.50, a $2 Rioja, or a $3 California Cabernet Sauvignon may not represent the best of each appellation, but it may nevertheless be a good value compared to many other red wines for the same price. There are few dry white wines that have much to recommend them except a fresh, clean taste. A $6 Chablis Premier Cru may well have more body and character than a $2.75 Muscadet, but what is their comparative value as dry white wine? You may find an Alsatian Sylvaner or certain California Chablis at $2 to be just as attractive as a $3 Soave, a château-bottled Graves at $3.50, or a $4 Neuchâtel from Switzerland. As for sweetness, it makes a cheap wine more appealing by masking its qualities: there is no reason to pay a high price for most semisweet rosés, or for many mellow whites either, unless they are wines with a distinct personality.

The price of wine is increasing steadily, but fortunately there is a greater variety of inexpensive wines in this country than anywhere else in the world. Most Europeans, for example, find it difficult to buy wines from any country other than their own, and it is not always easy for someone living in one wine region to find wines from another region within his own country. In most

American cities, however, an adventuresome consumer can buy wines from fifteen or twenty countries. In addition, importers are constantly expanding the range of their offerings among inexpensive wines, and American wineries are continually increasing the quality and distribution of their wines.

In addition to the wines described in this book, there are many attractive and inexpensive wines that are still comparatively hard to find. Those from small California wineries will always be in short supply, but you may come across such interesting imports as Lago di Caldaro and Pinot Grigio from northern Italy; Merlot del Ticino from Switzerland; Ruster Spätburgunder from Austria; Cabernet and Tamianka from Bulgaria; Tarnave Perla from Romania; and Australian Moselle. Algeria and Argentina both produce a tremendous amount of sound red wines which are bound to become more widely seen here.

There are as many different wines as there are grapes and plots of land on which to grow them, and it is this diversity which intrigues some and discourages others. Although wine can be enjoyed casually and without effort, it is not always the wine that comes most easily to hand that is the best value. This guide is an attempt to convey useful information about the best-known wines and, more importantly, to suggest new areas of exploration for those who want to drink good wine without paying too much for it.

Part I: The Approach to Inexpensive Wines

Retail Wine Prices

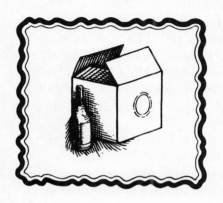

The prices cited in this book are those prevailing in New York City in the summer of 1973. Some prices will already have changed since then, of course, and others may increase in the near future. It is nevertheless fair to assume that as wine prices increase, they will do so in proportion to each other. The general guidelines established here will continue to be valid, as it is unlikely that the wines of Spain or Yugoslavia will become more expensive than those of the Côte de Nuits in Burgundy, that Muscadet will overtake Pouilly-Fuissé, or that California Burgundy will cost more than Cabernet Sauvignon.

Prices in certain cities may be higher or lower than those in New York, but the best values among the wines of the world will maintain their comparative position wherever they are sold in the United States. Part of the price variation from one state to another is the result of local taxes on table wines—all still, natural wines that contain no more than 14 percent alcohol. State taxes on table wines vary from virtually nothing in California, 2 cents a bottle in New York and Louisiana, 4 cents or 5 cents in Texas, Colorado, Connecticut, and Illinois, to as much as 22 cents in Florida and 30 cents in Georgia. Sparkling wines, such as Champagne and Sparkling Burgundy, and fortified wines, such as Sherry and Port, are subject to higher Federal taxes and usually, although not always, to higher state taxes as well.

Variations in state taxes and in the cost of inland freight account for only part of the difference from one state to another in the price of specific wines. For one thing, wholesale and retail markups vary to some extent from state to state. For another, some states control the retail price of wine, others do not. In a number of states the price of most branded wines is maintained by fair trade laws: the minimum retail price of various wines is established by the importer or wholesaler and filed with the state liquor authorities. When a wine is fair-traded, it will sell for the same price throughout the state, except for the occasional retailer who chooses to charge his inattentive customers an even higher price.

Even states that maintain fair-trade prices for wines nevertheless permit wholesalers to set the minimum resale price at the retailer's cost, thus effectively permitting each retailer to determine his own shelf price. While this may occasionally result in competitive pricing for established brands, it is more often small wholesalers specializing in very cheap wines who will permit a retailer to set his own price. In the absence of an established fair-trade price, retailers are free to increase their normal markup, which is usually 50 percent of their cost. Thus, if two Beaujolais are displayed side by side at $3 and $2.50 respectively, the first may be an established brand that costs the retailer $2, the other a wine of anonymous origin that costs $1.25 or less. Not only is the second wine not necessarily a good value—it may not even be a good wine, since its original cost is so low.

In cities without fair-trade laws, the price for any given wine may vary from one store to another on the same block. The difference is based not only on the competitive attitude of each retailer, but also on his ability to buy in large quantities, which will result in a lower cost. In contrast, if a retailer in a fair-trade state takes advantage of a wholesaler's special price reduction on a fair-traded wine, his retail profit will be bigger, but the price to the consumer remains the same.

There are two additional aspects of wine distribution that affect the range of wines available in certain stores, and the prices at which they are sold. One of them is referred to as "direct import." Legally a retailer cannot import wines directly (except in Washington, D.C.), but he can usually find a wholesaler who will waive his usual markup on large shipments in exchange for a small clearance fee. Consequently, a retailer who commits himself to sizable amounts of wine can obtain wines not available from his local wholesalers. These may be less familiar wines, or they may be such wines as Beaujolais and Liebfraumilch imported with the retailer's private label. He may also bring in special purchases of the famous châteaux of Bordeaux, German wines from the best estates, estate-bottled Burgundies, and other expensive wines of established reputation and value, which he can then offer at very competitive prices.

Another factor that affects local wine values is that of retail exclusivity. An importer or a California winery distributes its wines through normal wholesale channels in most cities, but may occasionally grant exclusive marketing rights in a particular city to a leading retailer or retail

THE APPROACH TO INEXPENSIVE WINES

chain. The reason is simply that in certain cities there are retailers who can do more business, given the incentive, than any available wholesaler. In return for large commitments and aggressive promotion, the retailer obtains the brand at a lower cost, once again bypassing the normal wholesale markup. It is therefore possible to buy wines from a particular California winery for considerably less in Boston than in San Francisco, or to buy a nationally distributed brand of imported wine for less in Milwaukee, St. Louis, or Denver than in New York, Chicago, or Los Angeles.

Buying Wine

Not long ago I visited a large liquor store with an extensive selection of wines. The manager strongly recommended a particular bottle of wine, describing in some detail its perfumed bouquet, its distinct and full-bodied character, and its lingering aftertaste. I asked him, in passing, if he had actually tasted the wine.

"No," he admitted, "but I've been meaning to."

The best way to buy wines, we are often told, is to find a reputable wine merchant and to trust his recommendations. This is excellent advice in theory, but finding a wine merchant, or even a helpful clerk, can be difficult in this country, where wine has traditionally been a minor part of the liquor business, and where salesmen tend to be less knowledgeable and more insistent than those so fondly recalled by English wine writers. Many liquor-store owners readily understand that wine is a blind item —that is, one without a clearly established value—and that they can make more profit on a bottle of wine than on a competitively priced bottle of whiskey that sells for twice as much. Some retailers have gone on to learn about wine, and can offer a well-chosen selection of wines at various prices. Many others simply display the most popular brands, plus a number of unfamiliar labels which they have bought cheaply and sell at a substantial markup.

Although this guide includes a great many specific recommendations, many of which can be found even in a small shop or—in states that permit it—on supermarket shelves, if you drink wine regularly and want both value and variety, it is well worth your time to seek out the best stores in your city. The bigger the selection, and the more knowledgeably it has been chosen, the more chance you have of finding some of the less-familiar wines mentioned in this guide. Furthermore, a big retailer is more likely to have an interesting choice of dependable private-label wines, with which you can experiment, than is the small retailer down the street. He may also have available one or more national brands on an exclusive basis, as described in the previous section. Finally, you will want to buy expensive wines from time to time, including Bordeaux châteaux, individual vineyard wines from Burgundy and from Germany, and wines from small California wineries with limited production. Only certain retailers will have a good selection of these wines, and they may also be priced lower than those available at the nearest liquor store.

Many stores issue catalogs periodically or advertise in the newspaper, which permits you to study their selection at leisure, and also to get some idea of what is being charged for various wines in your city. All too often, however, newspaper ads list wines such as Chablis, Chianti, Liebfraumilch, and Beaujolais without indicating a

shipper or brand name, so that there is no way to compare prices or to determine the real value of the wines
offered.

When you visit a store, try to determine whether the
owner take wines seriously, or simply stocks wine as a
necessary part of his liquor business. Are bottles kept on
their sides? Are the wines arranged in some kind of order
that helps you find what you want? Are wines available
from a great many regions at different price levels, or
does the store feature inexpensive versions of a few well-
known wine names? A cheap Beaujolais, Pouilly-Fuissé,
Châteauneuf-du-Pape, or Valpolicella is less of a value
than correctly priced wines from Spain, Yugoslavia,
Chile, and so on. Is there a good selection of California
wines, or just a few examples from the best-known wineries? Are there too many of the famous wines from Bordeaux, Burgundy, and Germany in off years, and are they
overpriced? Vintage charts, whatever their shortcomings,
will at least indicate the worst recent years in each major
wine region. There should be some choice of fine wines
in good vintages; even though these are necessarily expensive, their presence suggests that the retailer is aware
of them and wants to make them available to his customers. As a matter of fact, the classified châteaux of Bordeaux, most of which can be bought from several wholesalers at different prices, are a good indication of how
carefully a retailer shops, and how competitive he wants
to be. Are the vintages of inexpensive wines recent, or
does there seem to be a slow turnover? This is particularly important, because it will in turn determine the
freshness of nonvintage wines, those which do not carry
a vintage year on the label. Even an indifferent retailer
will remember that Beaujolais and Pouilly-Fuissé should
be drunk young, and will make sure that he doesn't have

four- or five-year-old examples on hand. Few are likely to pay the same attention to California wines, many of which are nonvintage, or to wines from unusual places whose vintages may not be accurate.

Of course you will want to determine if there is anyone associated with the store who can help you select a few bottles and who can guide you to unusual values. It may be the owner, his wine manager, or a clerk who is interested in wine, but unless there is someone who knows wines in general and his own stock in particular, you are not too likely to find the best values, if indeed there are any. Remember that even if the owner of a store has established a local reputation as a wine expert, he may not be around to help you choose, and his clerks may not know much more than the names of the wines they are expected to promote. Of course, every retailer features specific wines, and has instructed his staff accordingly. The extreme version of this occurs in some stores in Florida, where clerks are given as much as $1 a bottle to recommend certain wines, all of this amount charged to the customer.

Although there is no need to devote a great deal of time to finding one or two stores with a good and correctly priced selection, finding these is worth a little effort. Since you can buy several months' supply of wines at a time, the savings you realize by shopping around may be extensive. If there is not much choice in your town, a cooperative retailer can usually order wines in from another city within the state. He may have to buy a minimum of two or three cases, but as this may be the only way to get around a limited choice, you can arrange with friends to split the order.

Understanding Wine Labels

It has been my experience that people who don't know much about wine don't know what they like. Let me put this another way: Almost everyone who drinks a glass of wine is ready to voice an opinion, but many people have trouble recalling the wines they like best. Trying to remember what a wine label looks like is more difficult and less certain than simply remembering the name of the wine. This means being able to pick out the relevant words on a label.

Most wines are named after the place from which they come, usually a village or a district. France has hundreds of wine villages, including Châteauneuf-du-Pape, Pommard, St.-Emilion, Vouvray, Fleurie, Tavel, Chablis, and Sauternes; Soave, Bardolino, Barolo, Orvieto, and Frascati are villages in Italy; German villages include Bernkastel, Piesport, Johannisberg, Nierstein, and Rüdesheim; and other wine villages include Tokay in Hungary, Neuchâtel in Switzerland, Dão in Portugal, Gumpoldskirchen and Nussberg in Austria, and Valdepeñas in Spain.

Among the wines whose names are those of their district of origin are Beaujolais, Anjou, Côtes-du-Rhône, Médoc, Chianti, and Rioja. Geography is the key to understanding wines so labeled. If you can focus on the place of origin, rather than on the appearance of the label as a whole, and gradually build up a mental wine map for each country as you taste its wines, you will more easily recall the wines you enjoy.

The most specific place of origin of a wine is a vineyard, the specific plot of land from which it comes. Of course, every wine comes from a vineyard, but most of the world's wines are then blended together from many plots within a village, from several villages within a district, or from more than one district within a country. There are many vineyards throughout the world whose grapes are crushed, vinified, aged, and bottled apart from those of adjoining plots of land. Fortunately, individual vineyard wines usually have some indication on their labels of the district or village in which they are located. The most famous of these vineyards are in Bordeaux, Burgundy, and along the Rhine and Moselle, but most of them are well beyond our price limits.

A second way of labeling a wine is with the name of the grape variety from which it is made. This often occurs in wine regions without well-known villages or vineyards, so that the grape name is the closest that the producers can come to indicating the style of the wine in the bottle. Varietal labeling, as this is called, is widely used in California: Cabernet Sauvignon, Pinot Noir, Pinot Chardonnay, Zinfandel, and Grenache Rosé are among the best known California varietals. Some other varietal appellations are Gewürztraminer in Alsace; Lambrusco, Verdicchio, and Barbera in Italy; Fendant in Switzerland; and Chelois, Concord, and Catawba in New

York State. Sometimes a label will indicate both the wine's place of origin and the grape variety used: Bernkasteler Riesling, Cabernet of Istria, Debröi Hárslevelü, Monterey Riesling.

The major wine laws incorporate these two basic methods of labeling wines. France has created the laws of *Appellation Contrôlée*, that is, controlled appellation, or geographically delimited place names. Any wine subject to the *Appellation Contrôlée* laws—which include approximately the top 15 percent of the wines produced in France—must come from the village or district named on its label. *Appellation Contrôlée* is therefore an indication of origin, and the key word to look for on a French label is the one just above *Appellation Contrôlée* or between *Appellation* and *Contrôlée* because it tells you just where the wine comes from. These laws also specify the grape varieties permitted for that appellation (based on centuries of trial and error, and invariably the ones most suitable for that particular soil); minimum alcoholic content (to assure stability in poor years); maximum yield per acre (to prevent overproduction, which weakens the character of a wine); and other aspects of quality. Italian labels from the best districts increasingly carry the words *Denominazione di Origine Controllata,* as a guarantee that they conform to new laws similar in form and intent to the French laws. Italian wines may be named after the grapes from which they are made as well as from the place of origin, but even a wine named after a grape variety can come only from a specific delimited zone if its label bears the words *Denominazione di Origine Controllata.* German wines are all subject to that country's new wine laws, which are based on geographical origin, permitted grape varieties, and on just how ripe the grapes are when they are picked. These laws are described more fully in the section on Rhines and Moselles.

Most countries have wine laws, if not for all their wines, at least for those that they consider the best. The laws for each country may be more or less stringent as to the amount of wine from another region, from other grapes, or from other vintages that may be blended in with those of a particular appellation. They do codify the way wines are labeled, however, and therefore make it easier to recognize and recall specific wines.

Another popular way of marketing wines is with generic names, that is, by using the names of specific European wine districts that are already familiar to the consumer, such as Chablis, Burgundy, Chianti, Sauternes and Rhine Wine. A Spanish Burgundy, California Chablis, or Australian Sauterne may have only a coincidental resemblance—if any—to its prototype, and this method of labeling, which has obvious commercial advantages, is perhaps the least useful for the consumer.

There are certain fantasy wine names—such as Liebfraumilch (milk of the blessed mother) and Lacrima Christi (tears of Christ)—which refer neither to the place of origin nor to the grape variety used. These colorful appellations may be more or less defined, however, by local wine laws.

Increasingly, wine producers are using proprietary wine names, created by themselves and used only for their own wines. Some are used for the wines of a particular district, others may be used for wines from anywhere within the producing country; but they do help a consumer to remember specific wines that he enjoys. Baroque, Rubion, Barenblut, Chateau La Salle, Lake Country Red, Lake Roselle, del Magnifico, Blue Nun, Brillante, Viña Pomal, Mouton-Cadet, and Prince Noir are among the best known proprietary names.

Vintages

Vintage years are less important for most of the world's wines than consumers imagine, but more complicated for the finest wines than retailers let on. The wines of each vintage in every wine-producing region will differ to some extent from one year to the next. Even in regions where the weather is fairly constant year after year, variations during the growing cycle will affect the quantity produced, if nothing else, which will in turn affect the price of that wine. When judging quality, however, certain factors should be considered in order to put vintage dates into a proper perspective. How accurate is the label? How useful is the information? How important is the vintage when choosing one or another specific wine?

If a vintage year is inaccurate, it would be a mistake—to put it mildly—to use it as a guide to buying wines. If a California wine bears a vintage date, no more than 5 percent of wines from another vintage can be blended in. In Germany, only 75 percent of the year on the label need be used. In France, the figure is 100 percent, but inasmuch as vintage years are not a part of the *Appellation Contrôlée* laws, but of another set of laws, vintage dates are perhaps not so strictly enforced for lesser wines. In many other countries, vintage years are not taken seriously at all, and each producer or shipper will decide whether or not to blend together the wines of several vintages, and whether his wines will be dated chronologically or whimsically. In some wine regions, shippers who do not normally vintage-date their wines are happy to do so for their American importers, who in turn suggest a suitable year to use.

Even when vintages are accurately stated, how useful is the information? We may remember something about recent vintages in Bordeaux, Burgundy, and the Rhine, but which were the most successful years for Bardolino or Barolo, for Rioja or Valdepeñas, for Australia's Barossa Valley, the Dalmatian coast of Yugoslavia, or, if it comes to that, for Pinot Chardonnay from the Napa Valley or Cabernet Sauvignon from Monterey?

Fortunately, there are some general guidelines that simplify the problem of vintages, if only by suggesting large areas where it is not a critical factor. To begin with, it is well to remember that all rosés, almost all white wines, and many light red wines are best consumed soon after they are available. Additional aging in bottle will not improve them, and will in fact gradually diminish their appealing charm and freshness. For uncomplicated wines such as these—which includes most of the inexpensive wines described in this book—an accurate vintage year on the label is more useful as a guide to the age of a wine than to its quality. A one- or two-year-old white wine or rosé is almost always preferable to one that is three or four years old, even if the older vintage has a better reputation.

Another useful consideration when choosing less expensive wines is that vintages are much less important for a shipper's regional wine than for the wines of individual vineyards or estates. In Bordeaux, for example, the château wines—the unblended product of a particular plot of land—will vary more from year to year than will the regional blends of the various shippers. Not only do shippers tend to market the wines of good vintages only, but in blending their wines they invariably remove some of the character and personality of the vintage, so that there is a greater continuity of style and consistency of taste from year to year. This is not to say, by any means, that shippers' wines are of higher quality than those of individual vineyards, but rather that the vintage year on the label is not as important as, for example, the reputation of the shipper.

As a general rule, then, vintage years are more important for expensive wines than for cheaper wines. An expensive wine is more likely to come from one of the best vineyards or wine villages, whose fame and value is based to a large extent on what it is capable of producing with optimum weather conditions. At this level of excellence—which includes the finest white wines of Germany, Burgundy, and Sauternes, the red wines of Bordeaux, Burgundy, and northern Italy, and the best California varietal wines from a few top wineries—vintages really do matter. Major variations in the weather may occur each year, and this affects not only the quality and longevity of the wine, but very often the price at which it is sold as well. Unfortunately, vintages at this level matter so much that you cannot know just a little; you must know a lot.

We are now considering wines priced beyond the limits of this book, but to take an example, although 1964 red Bordeaux received a great deal of favorable publicity, in the Médoc the 1962s are often sounder wines and more consistently good. On the other hand, in St.-Emilion and Pomerol 1964 was a very good year indeed, and more successful than the 1962s. To take another example, 1970 Bordeaux are considerably better than the 1969s, but in Burgundy 1969 was an excellent year for red wines, which are somewhat better than the 1970s. On the other hand, white Burgundies were considered finer in 1970 than in 1969. Furthermore, the intrinsic quality of a fine red wine must be put into another context—its longevity and the rate at which it will mature. At any given time a good wine may be more appealing than an excellent wine that has been uncorked too soon, when it is still comparatively hard and tannic.

All these contradictory details are not meant to discourage anyone from learning about vintages. On the contrary, they underline the fact that when you pay $10 or more for a bottle of wine, it is a mistake to rate vintages as good and bad in too simple a way. Remember also that the vintages that are most often publicized, and that stick in the mind, usually represent successes in Bordeaux and Burgundy. Quality varies from one French district to another; French vintages do not usually have much in common with those in Germany; neither has much in common with what happens in Spain and Italy; and none of them has any relevance to the most successful years in northern California.

California vintages require a special comment. It has long been claimed that there are no bad vintages in California, and that every year is the same. The first claim is not far from the truth. Whereas poor weather in European districts may result in unripe grapes and weak wines, it is rare for grapes not to ripen in California. That does not mean, however, that every year is similar in style or equally good, as anyone can attest who has tasted a particular varietal wine from a single winery in two or three vintages. Furthermore, the weather sequence in any given summer will affect each grape variety differently: when several varieties are planted side by side, they cannot all be equally successful during the same summer.

There is surely nothing to be gained by suggesting that inexpensive Chablis and Burgundy sold in gallon jugs should be made from a single year's grapes. For more expensive wines, however, there is at least one good reason for putting a vintage on the label: it gives the consumer some idea of how old the wine is, which is especially useful for white wines and rosés. One tip that may be of use to you is that very often the bottom of the bottles used for California wines contain, among other markings, a two-digit number that corresponds to the last two digits of the year of manufacture. Since wineries have no reason to store empty bottles, you can assume that the wine was bottled in the year that the bottle was made. Some wineries have asked their glass suppliers to make the code less obvious, but many have not, so that you get at least some idea of how long ago a wine was bottled when buying nonvintage wines.

Vintage charts with numerical ratings can be of some use if you bear in mind that they cannot take into account any of the complexities suggested above, and that they are more useful for fine wines than for less expensive, blended wines. Also, the ratings tend to be more accurate for very good and very bad years: the middle range usually tells you more about the chartmaker's inventory than about the years in question. In fact, recent vintages are generally rated more generously than older ones; as the inventory goes down, so does the rating.

Tasting Wine

Some years ago I dined in an elaborately decorated and expensive restaurant in Atlanta. I was so surprised to see *gazpacho* on the menu that I ordered it, and this cold soup was beautifully served in a silver tureen, accompanied by minced onion and croutons. As I began to eat the soup, I had the most peculiar impression about its taste, which was later confirmed by a friendly waiter: I was sitting a long way from home, eating canned tomato juice out of a bowl with a spoon.

If there is any lesson to be learned from this incident, it is to trust your own reaction to whatever you taste. The extent to which many people are intimidated about their ability to judge wine was brought home to me when a successful importer explained his sales technique to me.

"When I offer a customer a sample of wine," he said, "I make sure to taste it before he does, and immediately pronounce it 'excellent.' The most he can do after that is demote it to 'very good.'"

Attentive tasting is usually confined to occasions when fine wines are being served, and the participants search for adjectives appropriate to the reputation of the wines. When inexpensive wines are being tasted, however, it is best to begin by asking, Is there anything wrong with this wine? It is less a search for the right word than it is a concern with self-preservation. The difficulty, and the challenge, of discovering good values among inexpensive wines is that you are usually dealing with wines that do not have established credentials. Either they are less familiar examples from major regions, or they are among the wines now being imported from wine regions and from countries whose wines were not previously seen here. Since you cannot react with certainty to an unfamiliar label, you are forced to react to the wine itself. For this reason, making an effort to taste wines carefully seems to me much more important for inexpensive and unfamiliar wines than for classic wines whose price and fame create pleasurable anticipation before they are even poured.

If you agree that inexpensive wines should be tasted even more critically than others, because the variation in quality is likely to be greater, then you should get into the habit of making some kind of tasting notes. It is probable that most of the people who bother to make notes on the wines they taste—professionals aside—are those who normally drink fine wines and want to recollect nuances of taste among different vineyards and vintages. It seems to me even more useful for the consumer of inexpensive wines to note down his impressions, and above all, to make sure he has written out the exact names of the wines he likes. A wine buff is more likely to remember the difference between two vintages of Château Lafite-Rothschild than the casual wine drinker is to remem-

THE APPROACH TO INEXPENSIVE WINES

ber the producer of a Rioja, Muscadet, Soave, Chenin Blanc, or Bordeaux Rouge that he enjoyed, and the latter wine drinker has much more to gain. When you come across a good wine you will want to buy more of it, and you should therefore get in the habit of keeping track of the wines you drink. The simplest way to do this is by keeping a small notebook in which you mark down the date; the name of the wine and the vintage; the producer, winery, or brand; the cost; and your comments. You may also want to put down where, or with whom, you drank the bottle, which may help to recall your impressions of the wine. If possible, make your notes with the bottle in front of you, as it is very easy to forget the relevant details on a label. In any case, the sooner you can note down your impressions, the more accurate they will be.

As for the notes themselves, they need not be elaborate. Try to define each wine in terms of its taste instead of personalizing it with such terms as charming, frivolous, friendly, unassuming, and so on. Also, make every effort to describe the wine itself, rather than your emotional reaction to it. Here, for example, is an English wine writer describing a thirty-year-old Burgundy: "I took one sip; I closed my eyes, and every beautiful thing that I had ever known crowded into my memory . . . the song of armies sweeping into battle, the roar of the waves upon a rocky shore, the glint of sunshine after rain on the leaves of a forest. . . ." Was this wine red or white?

When you taste an unfamiliar wine, you might begin by asking yourself some simple questions about it. Does it have any obvious faults—a strange or unpleasant bouquet, a spoiled or bitter taste? Is it dry, slightly mellow, or sweet? Is it neutral in taste, or distinct in some way? Is it delicate and light-bodied, or is it a big, full-flavored, and mouth-filling wine? If you have a dry white wine in front of you, is it crisp, with some refreshing acidity, or just an acceptable dull wine? If the wine is red, is it as good as it will ever be, or is there enough flavor and tannin to suggest it will improve with time? Is the wine long or short on your palate, which is to say, is the flavor so mild that you hardly have the sense of drinking wine, or does it have so much character that you continue to taste the wine even after you have swallowed it? These are questions that anyone can answer easily for himself, simply by dealing with them one at a time.

If you choose to taste wines more formally, you should approach each glass as does a professional taster, examining in turn a wine's color, bouquet, and taste. The color of a wine, that is, its hue, can tell you a lot about it, especially in a negative way. Red wines are red-purple in color at first and gradually fade with time to a pale red, and finally to a tawny color with a more or less brown tinge. The original hue of a white wine varies from an almost watery paleness to rich gold. As red wines lighten with age, so white wines darken, taking on a deeper cast, and finally turning an unattractive dark brown. With this in mind, the color of a wine will give you a good idea of the way it is aging, irrespective of the vintage year on its label. Color can be particularly important in evaluating inexpensive wines, since these are so often light wines that are meant to be consumed young and that do not age with much grace. Oxidized whites and fading reds are hardly a good value.

Although you can judge the brilliance and clarity of a wine by holding it up to a light, to judge its hue you must tip your glass away from you—against a white background—and examine the outer edge of the wine. If you look down into a glass of wine, the amount of wine it contains will alter its hue.

The bouquet of a wine is a more useful guide to its quality, particular characteristics, and faults than most people realize, because much of what we imagine to be taste is really smell. For example, a child holds his nose when he has to swallow medicine because he has learned that if he cannot smell it, he will not taste it. Furthermore, for most of us the sense of smell is more accurate and more evocative than the sense of taste. Whether it is the unpleasant prickly sensation that reveals an excess of sulfur, the vinegary smell that betrays a wine which is beginning to spoil, or the attractive and distinct character of such wines as Beaujolais, Moselle, and Cabernet Sauvignon, a wine's bouquet can tell you a great deal about the wine itself before you taste it. To smell a wine, gently swirl your half-filled glass; this permits some of the wine to evaporate against the sides of the glass, releasing its bouquet.

What you actually taste in a wine is, to a large extent, a combination of acidity, tannin, and the presence or absence of sweetness. Acidity is a necessary element in a soundly made wine. Too much will make a wine unpleasantly tart, too little makes it dull and neutral. White wines especially need acidity to give them a liveliness and freshness of taste.

Any young red wine that needs time to mature will exhibit the astringent, puckerish quality that reveals the presence of tannin. As a wine develops, the amount of tannin diminishes, and certain red wines that are well made to begin with will become softer and more appealing if they are given a year or two in bottle. In fact, the sediment found in older red wines is formed by the combination of tannin and coloring matter, which is why such wines are both lighter in color and softer in taste. Wines such as Beaujolais, Valpolicella, and most California Zinfandels do not have much tannin and can be consumed soon after they are bottled, as can all light red wines. On the other hand, tannin is normally present in red Bordeaux, many Chiantis, and Cabernet Sauvignon wines from California, Chile, and Yugoslavia, and these wines generally benefit from bottle age.

Although a number of table wines are more or less sweet, most of them are dry—that is, all of the sugar originally present in the juice has been converted by fermentation into alcohol. Nevertheless, some dry wines seem drier than others because they contain more acidity or tannin.

When you take your first sip of a wine, roll it around in your mouth for a moment so that all of the taste buds on your tongue are exposed to the wine. Professional tasters sometimes chew a wine to get it around their mouths, others whistle in, quickly drawing air into their mouths to intensify the taste of the wine. If you concentrate, it is not difficult to isolate the elements in a wine or to be aware of two or three tastes simultaneously. For example, red vermouth is normally quite sweet, but it also contains quinine, so that the first impression of sweetness is balanced by a certain bitterness. To take a more common example, lemonade is a simple combination of acidity and sweetness. Strong tea is a bitter solution dominated by tannin; if you add a slice of lemon you add acidity, and if you then add sugar to mask the first two elements, you have created a simple combination of sour, sweet, and bitter. These are the three elements you find in wine, although in a more subtle and better-balanced combination.

When a wine is in your mouth, you also become aware of its body in terms of its weight on your palate. It may be light and delicate, or full and rich, and its success in complementing various dishes has as much to do with this as with anything else.

Making notes whenever you can, or at least taking a few moments to isolate a wine's elements, forces you to concentrate on the wine and on what you think of it. If you keep a notebook or make notes on the blank pages of your calendar or address book, you will be surprised at how much easier it becomes to define your impressions, how much simpler it is to remember what you drink, and how much more you enjoy wine. And of course you will end up saving a great deal of money by going back to the wines you enjoy at the price you want to pay.

Storing and Serving Wine

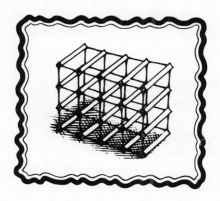

STORAGE An acquaintance who worked in a liquor store once showed me his wine cellar. One way or another he had managed to collect a great many different bottles from the store's inventory, and now that he was leaving the country he had decided to sell them.

"Suppose I offered to sell all these wines back to the owner of the store," he said to me. "What do you think he would give me for the entire lot?"

I looked at the floor-to-ceiling racks and said, "Twenty years."

Keeping a few bottles of wine on hand need not be so dangerous, and it will both save you money and increase your pleasure. Once you have determined some of your preferences and have found one or two dependable sources of wine, you will want to buy in larger quantities. Most stores offer a discount if you buy by the case of twelve bottles, and if you have a place to store wines you can also take advantage of special sales as they occur.

Whether you store a variety of wines or just a red and a white wine that you drink regularly, you will avoid the trouble and expense of having to buy at the last minute from a neighborhood store whose selection may be limited and overpriced.

There is another good reason for finding a place to keep wines, which is that many red wines improve with bottle age. This is especially true of the finer Bordeaux and Burgundies that are outside the scope of this book, but certain inexpensive wines will also improve with six months or a year in bottle. In fact, while a fine Bordeaux that costs $8 or $10 may need five years or more for its best qualities to develop, a $2 or $3 red wine may improve tremendously within a year or so, enabling you to drink a mature wine without having spent much money for it.

If you put together more than a few bottles, it is a good idea to keep a record of what you have on hand. Otherwise you may forget about certain good bottles that you have put aside for an occasion. More importantly, you may forget about inexpensive white wines and rosés for months at a time, while they lose some of their charm and appeal. The simplest way to keep track of what you own is to get an itemized bill—insist that it be legible—whenever you buy a selection of wines. This gives you, on one piece of paper, the names and vintage years of the wines (fill in whatever is left out by the clerk), the price, where you bought the wines, and when. As you drink these wines, mark your comments directly on the bill. This is the simplest way to remember what you own, and what you thought of the wines you have already drunk. You may also find it useful to mark down the purchase date on the labels of nonvintage wines that you don't plan to drink immediately.

The best place to store wines is in a cool place, or at least in a corner where the temperature does not fluctuate from day to day. Bottles should be kept on their sides so that the cork stays wet and expanded, thereby preventing air from getting at the wine. Whiskey cartons placed on their sides provide the least expensive way to store wines. If you buy wine racks, make sure they are stackable, so that you can expand your cellar if you choose to.

CORKSCREWS You only buy a corkscrew once, so it may as well be a dependable one. A good corkscrew has a long bore—at least two inches long—so that it can penetrate the long corks used for good bottles of wine. The bore should be in the form of a true coil, not a wiggly line that resembles an awl. A coil will get a good grip even on a bad cork, rather than simply drilling a hole in it. The easiest corkscrews to use are those that have some kind of leverage mechanism, so that you do not have to tug at a cork that is firmly embedded in its bottle. If you break a cork as you are trying to extract it, the best procedure is to start again at an angle to get a fresh grip on the remaining piece, instead of just making the existing hole bigger.

GLASSES Wineglasses are traditionally stemmed and are made of clear glass, so that a wine's color and appearance can be easily discerned. The bowl should be large enough—say, 8 to 12 ounces—so that the glass need only be filled halfway, permitting you to swirl the wine to release its bouquet. The bowl should also be slightly tapered, to retain the wine's bouquet. An all-purpose glass, whether it has a round bowl or one that is tulip-shaped, will do for all table wines. If you have two sets of wineglasses, it is traditional to use the smaller ones for white wines. If you ever plan to serve two red wines or two white wines together for purposes of comparison, you will find it less confusing to serve them in two differently shaped glasses.

TEMPERATURE   White wines and rosés are chilled before they are served; two hours in a refrigerator or twenty minutes in any bucket or pot filled with ice and water will do the trick. A white wine that is not cool enough will lose much of its appeal; it will taste neutral, rather than crisp and fresh. Any wine that is too cold will have very little taste at all. Overchilling expensive wines, as is often done in restaurants, robs you of the quality for which you are paying; overchilling very cheap white wines and rosés is occasionally to be recommended.

Red wines taste best at cool room temperature. Whatever the temperature of the dining room or terrace, a red wine should never taste warm on your tongue. Light reds can be cooled down for 15 minutes in the refrigerator, so that they are served at what would be cellar temperature if we still had cellars.

BREATHING   In the fall of 1964, I was passing by a retail liquor store when the owner came rushing out, announced that he had an emergency call from one of his best wine customers, and asked me to come along as consultant. As we rode our taxi to a Fifth Avenue cooperative, he explained that his customer had just opened two double magnums (each equal to four bottles) of Château Lafite-Rothschild 1961, for which he had paid $75 each, and had found the wine sour. We arrived to find the dining table set for sixteen, the two double magnums open on the sideboard, and the host completely distraught. We tasted the wine and found, not surprisingly, that it was quite tannic but perfectly sound; it was simply being served at least ten years too soon. Just then the hostess came running in and announced that it was all a false alarm because her Italian maid had just tasted the wine and found it every bit as good as the wines she was used to drinking in Naples. At this point, thinking of guests whose palates may have been formed on wines less astringent, I suggested that if the double magnums were decanted and the wine allowed to breathe, this exposure to air would soften it somewhat by the time it was served.

"Well, what are you waiting for?" the lady shouted at her husband. "You heard what he said. Make it breathe. Make it breathe."

Even if you drink less than $150 worth of wine at a time, you will find that most red wines improve to a greater or lesser extent if they are exposed to air for a while before being served. Any mustiness that may be present will disappear, the wine's bouquet will develop, and the tannic astringency typically found in many young red wines will be softened. The usual way to let a wine breathe is to uncork it thirty minutes or an hour before it is to be poured, but this is actually the least effective way to accomplish the purpose. In a restaurant, where you cannot wait for an hour while the wine breathes in its bottle, ask to have the wine poured into large glasses as soon as it is brought to your table. The most effective way to allow a wine to breathe, however, is to decant it.

DECANTING   To decant a wine you simply pour it from its bottle into any clean container, whether it is a crystal decanter, an attractive pitcher, a carafe, or another bottle. Decanting is usually practiced in the case of fine old red wines which have thrown a deposit. If the bottle is allowed to stand for a couple of hours so that the sediment falls to the bottom, and then carefully decanted in one continuous motion, the sediment will be left behind in the original bottle. Few inexpensive wines are likely to have sediment, but any number of inexpensive red wines will benefit by the exposure to air that is inherent in decanting. If you decant into a container not often used, you may want to rinse it out first with a few drops of wine to remove any off-odor or mustiness that would otherwise affect the wine itself.

Decanting into carafes is also a good idea when you serve wines from gallon jugs, not so much to improve the wine, but because it is so much easier to pour wine from a carafe than from a heavy jug when you are seated.

LEFTOVER WINE White wines and rosés should be put back in the refrigerator. Red wines should ideally be put in a cool place; otherwise these should be refrigerated as well. You might want to take a leftover red wine out of the refrigerator half an hour before serving it, so that it is not too cold to taste. The most important fact to remember, however, is that it is an excess of air that turns wine sour. Cork up leftover wine as soon as possible, rather than leaving a half-empty bottle standing for hours on the dining table before putting it away. If a wine begins to taste sharp, you can add soda water and make a *spritzer*, or add sugar and slices of fruit to make Sangria. You should never cook with a wine that has turned sour —the alcohol evaporates and only the taste remains—unless you are in the habit of using vinegar when a recipe calls for wine.

WINE AND FOOD During a visit to the Sauternes district, I once complimented the cellar master of a famous château on his wine and made the obvious remark that it would be a wonderful match with a rich dessert.

"Dessert?" he asked, offended. "Why, this wine would be excellent with chicken, with beef, with fish. And with Roquefort cheese, superb."

In matching wine and food, more than one person has made a virtue of necessity, and in many wine regions the choice is more often dictated by the wines available than by traditional rules. It is worth noting, however, that fish brings out a bitter metallic taste in red wines, that the acidity in salad dressing brings out an excess acidity in wine, and that rich dishes will overwhelm light-bodied wines. I think most people would privately agree that the choice of color is easily determined by the meal and personal preference, but that exactly which red or white wine is served depends more on the importance of the guests than on the taste of the food.

Part II: The Wines

Red Wines

FRANCE

Beaujolais

Beaujolais may well be the best-selling imported dry red wine in this country, and, along with Chianti, the wine most readily available in stores and restaurants. At its best, this wine is among the most agreeable in the world: its red-purple color, its distinct and perfumed bouquet, and its fresh and slightly grapey flavor all contribute to its tremendous popularity. More charming than a Rhône, more enjoyable than many a fine Burgundy, and more appealing than a young Bordeaux, Beaujolais is the perfect example of a casual wine that does not require attentive sipping.

Unfortunately, the price of Beaujolais has increased to the point where it can no longer be bought and drunk so casually. Beaujolais from major shippers now costs $3 to $4, and a wine such as Moulin-à-Vent may cost more than

$6. This seems a high sum to pay for a wine whose greatest virtue is its charm and lack of complexity, all the more so since Beaujolais is the kind of wine that is usually consumed in large quantities. Even though good Beaujolais can no longer be considered inexpensive, it is such a unique and delightful wine that you may choose to ignore comparative value in this case. There are so many different labels of Beaujolais available, however, that there is good reason to examine this popular wine with some attention.

About half of the wine produced annually in the Beaujolais region—which extends from Mâcon to Lyon in southern Burgundy—comes from the southernmost part and is entitled only to be called Beaujolais or **Beaujolais Supérieur**. The primary difference between the two appellations is that Beaujolais must have a minimum alcoholic content of 9 percent, and Beaujolais-Supérieur of 10 percent. Since it would be difficult indeed to find a Beaujolais in this country with less than 11 percent, this distinction is virtually meaningless to us. As a matter of fact, less than 5 percent of the Beaujolais crop is declared by the winemaker as Beaujolais-Supérieur: its appearance on a label here is largely gratuitous.

Of the remaining 50 percent of production, about half is made up of **Beaujolais-Villages**, which comes from thirty-five villages in central Beaujolais whose individual names are rarely seen on a label, but whose wine is presumably better than that simply called Beaujolais. The last 25 percent comes from nine villages to the north: **Brouilly, Fleurie, Moulin-à-Vent, Morgon, St.-Amour, Chénas, Juliénas, Chiroubles,** and **Côte de Brouilly.** They are sometimes referred to—unofficially—as the *grands crus* of Beaujolais, and are capable of producing the best wines of the region. Of the nine villages, Fleurie, Brouilly, and Moulin-à-Vent make up half the total production, and these are the village appellations most often seen here.

There is, naturally enough, an increase in price and a theoretical increase in quality as you progress up the scale of appellations from Beaujolais to Beaujolais-Villages and then to the wines of the nine individual villages. In actual fact, however, the differences in the wines that should normally result from the variations in the soil from which they come is subject to two undermining factors. The first is that there is more than one style of Beaujolais; the second is that there is a lot of Beaujolais available that does not taste like Beaujolais.

The style of Beaujolais that has long been popular within the region, in the restaurants of Lyon, and in the bistros of Paris is called Beaujolais *primeur*. It is typically fresh, light-bodied, and meant to be consumed young. In fact, it usually makes its first appearance on French restaurant tables within six weeks of the vintage, often served directly from barrels into open carafes. Although there is an increasing vogue for months-old Beaujolais in this country, a true Beaujolais *primeur* is not meant either to travel or to age. If you can get such a Beaujolais in a local shop in the late winter or early spring following a vintage, by all means try a bottle, but don't put it aside for the following winter. Some of the young Beaujolais that is shipped here is labeled Beaujolais *nouveau,* and is similar in style to a *primeur*. Beaujolais *de l'année* (of the year) simply indicates that the wine is of the most recent vintage, and should theoretically be sold only until the next vintage is available.

Most of the Beaujolais shipped here, however, is of another kind. It should still retain the fruit and appeal typical of Beaujolais, but it will be a wine with more body, some of its fruit muted, and with perhaps more style than charm. The commercial rationale of making a longer-lived wine is obvious, since the wines of any given vintage will continue to be stocked on retail shelves for two or three years. This also means that there are many examples of Beaujolais, well made and unmistakably genuine, that do not have quite the style of the wines drunk in the region. This cannot be said, for example, of a fine Bordeaux or Burgundy, and therefore suggests that despite its great popularity Beaujolais does not travel quite so well as do many other wines. People who complain that no wine tastes as good as on its home ground are often wrong, but in the case of Beaujolais the complaint may be valid.

In addition to Beaujolais that has lost some of its charm, there is a more serious problem, and that is Beaujolais that does not taste like Beaujolais. There are two reasons for this. One is that Beaujolais is one of the few important wines of France whose price is still determined, to some extent, by alcoholic degree. The price for inexpensive blending wines is determined by a combination of current market value multiplied by the alcoholic degree of the wine, which is logical enough when alcoholic content is the only difference between two nondescript wines. The result of using this formula for Beaujolais, however, is that most producers, large and small, add sugar to the fermenting must to increase the alcoholic content of their wines by one or two degrees. Chaptalization, as this is called, is valid in poor vintages when a wine might otherwise not contain enough alcohol to make it stable. If chaptalization is carried out in good years as well, however, its effect on wines noted primarily for their charm is obvious, and the result is a great deal of rather dull and heavy wine.

The other reason is that wines from the south are often added to Beaujolais by less scrupulous shippers to add body, color, and alcoholic degree, and also, of course, to lower their costs. The result is a wine that may be pleasant enough but that is not Beaujolais.

If Beaujolais cost $2 or less, these uncharacteristic wines would be unfortunate but perhaps not so serious a problem for the consumer. It seems absolutely pointless, however, to pay $3 or $4 a bottle for a wine with a unique style and end up with an undistinguished red wine with some body but without a personality of its own. If you want a pleasant light red wine, there are plenty of examples described in this book for $2.50 or less. Why pay more? On the other hand, if you enjoy Beaujolais, you must now be prepared to spend a bit more and to choose carefully, not only to avoid the stretched wines, but equally importantly to avoid the heavy-bodied and dull wines that many consumers associate with the name Beaujolais.

Beaujolais is available from a great number of shippers located throughout France, who buy their wines from the thousands of small properties throughout the region, and also from the cooperative cellars that now account for about half of the annual production. There are certain small estates that bottle their own wines, as well as a number of fairly large properties—some of them bigger than the famous châteaux of Bordeaux—whose wines are found here. There are good and bad examples to be found from all three sources, and since Beaujolais is a wine whose overall style is more important than are the individual characteristics of a particular vineyard, the virtues of estate-bottled wines are less relevant in Beaujolais than in the Côte de Nuits and the Côte de Beaune. The best approach to Beaujolais is to try several wines of the most recent vintage—both Beaujolais and Beaujolais *grands crus*—to find a good wine at a reasonable price, and then to drink that wine until the next good vintage comes along. The selection that follows does not include the least expensive Beaujolais available, but rather several dependable wines that will serve as a useful standard when you try less expensive examples available locally. You will find that not infrequently village wines such as Brouilly, Fleurie, or Morgon are only a little more expensive than a simple Beaujolais from a major shipper, and as such, comparatively good value. Among the shippers who produce sound Beaujolais are Jadot, Drouhin, Dulong, and Piat. The first two ship comparatively rich wines, whereas the St. André of Piat is lighter in style. Among the village wines, the Moulin-à-Vent of Jadot, Jaffelin, and the Château des Jacques of Thorin are big wines worth looking for. Other well-made wines include Prosper Maufoux Beaujolais-Brouilly, Brouilly Château des Tours, the Fleurie of Latour, and such wines as Chiroubles and Morgon from Loron, Frank Schoonmaker, and the Alexis Lichine Company.

Bordeaux Rouge
Médoc
St.-Emilion

Bordeaux produces many of the world's finest red wines, and its most famous vineyards are well known, at least by name, to wine drinkers everywhere. Among the thousands of Bordeaux vineyards, traditionally called châteaux, there are about a hundred that have been classified at one time or another in terms of their relative quality. These vineyards are known as *crus classés*, or classed growths: *cru*, or growth, is synonymous with vineyard and château. The classified châteaux, as they will be referred to here, include such famous vineyards as Lafite-Rothschild, Haut-Brion, Pétrus, Beychevelle, Lascombes, Palmer, Talbot, Cos d'Estournel, and so on. The prices of the classified châteaux have increased so much in the past two or three years, and with so much attendant publicity, that many consumers have concluded that they can no longer afford to drink the wines of Bordeaux. Despite their fame, however, the classified châteaux produce less than 3 percent of the region's wines. The rest of Bordeaux's vineyards, however, probably produce more red wines of good quality than any other region in the world, and these wines are so widely available in this country that they continue to provide good values. In order to buy Bordeaux wisely, it is necessary to separate its wines into three basic categories: the classified châteaux whose wines are now well beyond our price limits; the regional wines marketed by the many shippers of Bordeaux; and the individual wines of hundreds of lesser châteaux, often referred to as *petits châteaux*.

Although the classified châteaux have always received most of the attention of knowledgeable consumers and retailers, the biggest proportion of the wines of Bordeaux are marketed as regional blends by the various *négociants,* or shippers. Bordeaux Rouge is the basic appellation for this region, of course, and the principal inner districts for red wines are St.-Emilion, Pomerol, Graves, and the Médoc. The Médoc, in turn, contains the wine villages of Pauillac, St.-Estèphe, St.-Julien, and Margaux. Bordeaux Rouge, Médoc, and St.-Emilion are the most popular regional wines, and most shippers market all of them in this country. Many shippers also market a St.-Estèphe, St.-Julien, and Margaux. Some offer a regional Pauillac or

THE WINES

Pomerol, but Graves is very rarely seen as a regional red wine.

When making up a regional wine, each shipper buys wines in barrel from among the thousands of large and small properties that lie within the particular appellation that concerns him. He blends the wines of that year to produce the style of wine for which he is known, and which he thinks will most appeal to his clientele. Since regional wines are blended, they do not express the characteristics of a particular vintage as much as do the wines of a single property: a great year will seem less so in a regional wine; a moderate year will seem better than its reputation might suggest. In addition, shippers do not normally market the wines of poor years, at least not with those years on their labels, so that the reputation of the shipper is a more useful guide to the quality of a regional wine than is the vintage. Regional wines are meant to be consumed without much additional aging, and therefore lack the tannic backbone of finer—and more expensive—wines. While this means that a regional wine of a given vintage is always readier to drink than is a classified château, it also suggests that these wines do not age very well; the most recent available vintage will almost always be more appealing than an older one that you may come across.

Starting with the biggest of the regional appellations, more than half of the red wines of Bordeaux are sold with the appellation Bordeaux or Bordeaux Supérieur, and of course this is the common denominator for the wines of this region. The principal difference between the two appellations is that the first must have a minimum of 10 percent alcohol, the second 10½ percent. Since few Bordeaux are shipped into this country with less than 11 percent alcohol, the distinction is largely academic in terms of choosing one over the other. A wine labeled simply Bordeaux or Bordeaux Supérieur can come from anywhere in the region, and therefore quality within this appellation is likely to vary the most from one shipper to another. Because a shipper has so much latitude when he makes up a Bordeaux or Bordeaux Supérieur, inexpensive examples are unlikely to be particularly well made. As a matter of fact, this seems to hold true for more expensive appellations as well. Importers and wholesalers who specialize in very cheap wines, often sold under private labels, buy their wines entirely on price, often switching from one supplier to another every year. The result is not only a lack of continuity in the wine but also a tacit understanding between the supplier (whose name does not appear on the label) and the importer concerning the quality of the wine itself.

There are a couple of points worth noting about the way Bordeaux and Bordeaux Supérieur are marketed. The first is that some Bordeaux shippers market this appellation as a brand name, with the appellation itself less prominently displayed on the label. Club Claret of de Luze, Prince Noir of B&G, Monopole of Cruse, Camponac of Eschenauer, and Mouton-Cadet are some examples. The second point is that more Bordeaux shippers are now labeling this wine with the name of the grape variety, as is done for certain California wines. Cabernet de Bordeaux, Cabernet Sauvignon, and Cabernet-Merlot are three ways of labeling a Bordeaux: since Bordeaux vineyards are extensively planted in Cabernet Franc and Merlot, as well as Cabernet Sauvignon, Cabernet-Merlot is probably the most accurate way to label this wine.

Occasionally you will come across a wine that looks like a bottle of Bordeaux, and that may have been shipped from Bordeaux, but whose label does not contain the key words *Appellation Bordeaux Contrôlée,* which would signify that the wine is indeed a Bordeaux. A wine that comes from an established shipper, such as Plaisir de France of Cordier, or Grand Chartrons of Nathaniel Johnston, may be a fresh and drinkable red wine, but the quality of anonymous examples is less certain.

Moving up the scale from Bordeaux Rouge, the two best-known districts within Bordeaux are the Médoc and St.-Emilion. Although the Médoc produces more wine over all, more than half of it is sold under the more expensive village appellation of Margaux, St.-Julien, St.-Estèphe, Pauillac, and so on. As a result, there is actually more wine available to be marketed as St.-Emilion than as Médoc. The style of St.-Emilion, which is made primarily from the Merlot grape, is softer, rounder, and less tannic in character than the wines of the Médoc, with their high proportion of Cabernet Sauvignon grapes. As a group, the regional wines of St.-Emilion seem more successful than do the Médocs, and in addition their style makes them more appealing to many consumers.

If there were a direct correlation between the quality and the price of regional wines, it might work out as follows: Bordeaux Rouge, $3; Médoc and St.-Emilion, $3.50; and village appellations such as Margaux, St.-Julien, and St.-Estèphe, $4.50. The prices at which these wines are actually sold today, however, is more a reflection of what has been happening to the Bordeaux market than it is an expression of the value of the wines. For one thing, many shippers sell their Bordeaux for only a little less than their Médoc, which makes the latter a much better value. A St.-Emilion is generally only slightly more expensive than a Médoc, so if you prefer a softer wine, it's easily worth the extra money. The village appellations, on the other hand, are now selling for $5 to $8 each, not because the wines are that much better, but because they are now that much harder to buy from the vineyard proprietors. There are two reasons for this shortage of Margaux, St.-Julien, St.-Estèphe, and Pauillac. In the past, the excess production of classified châteaux in these villages was sold off under the appropriate appellation to be used in regional blends, but small crops of 1969 and 1971 resulted in a shortage of these appellations. Furthermore, many proprietors of small vineyards who previously sold off their wines in barrel to the shippers, have now taken to bottling their wines at the property and selling it under the château name. The incredible result is that regional Margaux and St.-Julien in barrel now costs the shippers as much as did the famous classified châteaux in bottle only two or three years ago.

The best approach for the consumer of regional wines to take is to concentrate on Médoc and St.-Emilion, to buy Bordeaux or Bordeaux Supérieur carefully, and to ignore the more expensive appellations entirely.

What follows is a short list of some dependable regional Bordeaux wines that are widely available and that can be used for comparison with less expensive private labels and *petits châteaux*. The basic difference in style among regional red Bordeaux—apart from those wines which are simply of poor quality—is between those with a certain amount of character and flavor, and those which are light, fresh, and comparatively soft. Those in the second group, which includes the wines of Sichel, Nathaniel Johnston, and Lavergne, are specifically vinified to retain less tannin: they have less of the traditional Bordeaux character, but will be more appealing to those who enjoy a softer wine.

B&G   Prince Noir (Bordeaux Supérieur)
             Médoc

Calvet	Médoc
Cordier	St.-Emilion
Cruse	La Dame Rouge (Médoc)
de Luze	Club Claret (Bordeaux)
	St.-Emilion
Ginestet	Haut-Médoc
	St.-Emilion
Johnston	Médoc
	St.-Emilion
Lavergne	Pavillon Rouge (Bordeaux)
Lichine	Médoc
Sichel	Cabernet-Merlot (Bordeaux)
	St.-Emilion

Petits Châteaux of Bordeaux

Apart from classified châteaux and regional wines, there is a third category of Bordeaux wines made up of hundreds of properties, each of whose wines is sold under the individual château name. There were always many proprietors among the less-renowned châteaux of Bordeaux who preferred to bottle their own wines in good vintages, and to sell them off in barrel to the shippers in poor vintages. In the past few years, however, the cachet of the words *mise en bouteille au château,* bottled at the property, has increased to such an extent on the American market that more and more vineyard owners have decided to bottle their own wines, and thus obtain a higher price for them. The fact that a wine has been bottled at the property by the man who made it can be a guarantee of the authenticity of a wine, but of course it is not necessarily a guarantee of its quality. When you buy expensive wines of high quality, such as those of the famous châteaux, you naturally want to be sure that you are getting an authentic wine. Whether it also makes sense for lesser vineyards to château-bottle their wines should depend entirely on the quality of the wines each one produces, but the vogue here for château-bottled wines is such that there are now hundreds of examples selling for $1.50 to $5. These wines are usually referred to as *petits châteaux*, which can be translated as lesser chateaux, since many of these properties are actually larger than the average classified châteaux.

Most importers now feature one or two *petits châteaux*, and some offer a dozen or more from different districts at different prices. Most of these wines bear the appellation Bordeaux or Bordeaux Supérieur. There are also some from St.-Emilion, from Graves, whose red wines are generally more successful than its whites, and from the Médoc villages of Listrac and Moulis, whose wines are less expensive than those of St.-Estèphe and Margaux. Some *petits châteaux* labels bear less familiar appellations of Bordeaux, such as Côtes de Bourg, Premières Côtes de Blaye, Premières Côtes de Bordeaux, Canon-Fronsac, Côtes de Fronsac, and so on. Wines from any of these districts could be sold simply as Bordeaux, and so it is particularly helpful to have additional information about the exact provenance of an individual wine. Bourg, Blaye, and Fronsac in particular produce some very attractive wines, not long-lived, but with more personality and charm than many regional blends.

The reasons for buying *petits châteaux* rather than regional wines are that they have more individuality, the capability to develop some style and finesse with a year or two in bottle, and often cost less. The reasons to proceed with caution are that many of them are nondescript, and some are in fact nonexistent: the château name is simply a brand name created by the shipper or importer, and therefore the wine is no different from a regional blend. In addition, since each *petit château* is sold exclusively by whichever importer brings it into the country, the price may be higher than the wine would normally warrant. A good way to shop for inexpensive châteaux is to buy a selection, invite a few friends over and taste them all together. You should be able to find, from among the wines available in your area, at least one that is good value for the present, and another that is worth putting away for a year.

This selection of *petits châteaux* includes wines priced from $2.50 to $4 that are distributed throughout the country. Some of the châteaux listed were officially classified as *crus bourgeois* in the nineteenth century, but price and quality are perhaps more relevant here than official rankings.

Château Timberlay (Bordeaux Supérieur)
Château Malbec (Bordeaux Supérieur)
Château de Terrefort-Quancard (Bordeaux Supérieur)
Château Cantegrive (Bordeaux Supérieur)
Château Guiraud-Cheval-Blanc (Côtes de Bourg)
Château Lauretan (Premières Côtes de Bordeaux)
Château Loudenne (Médoc)
Château Vieux Robin (Médoc)
Château Paveil-de-Luze (Haut-Médoc)
Château Patache d'Aux (Médoc)
Château l'Estage (Listrac-Médoc)
Château Sénéjac (Haut-Médoc)
Château Monbousquet (St.-Emilion)

Château Trimoulet (St.-Emilion)
Château Picque-Caillou (Graves)
Château Respide (Graves)

Bourgogne Rouge
Pinot Noir

Whether Bordeaux or Burgundy produces the finest wines of France is a question that serious wine drinkers have long debated, but at current prices most of us will have to argue the point from memory. The best wines from each region have always been expensive, but although regional wines and lesser chateaux from Bordeaux can still be bought for less than $3.50, it is almost impossible to buy anything but a Bourgogne Rouge for much less than $4.50.

The wines that have established the reputation of Burgundy throughout the world come from the Côte d'Or, a thirty-mile strip of vineyards south of Dijon which is divided into two sections, the Côte de Nuits and the Côte de Beaune. It is difficult to find wine from any of the best known villages along the Côte d'Or—Gevrey-Chambertin, Chambolle-Musigny, Vosne-Romanée, Nuits St.-Georges, Beaune, Pommard, or Volnay—for much under $6, and many examples now cost $9 or $10. Wines from such *grand cru* vineyards as Chambertin, Clos de la Roche, Bonnes-Mares, Musigny, Clos de Vougeot, Richebourg, and Corton cost $8 to $15 a bottle, and those from the most famous estates of all cost $15 to $40 a bottle for current vintages. The high cost of Burgundy results from several factors, the most important of which is that there is very little of it. All the red wine produced in the Côte de Nuits and the Côte de Beaune, for example, amounts to only half as much as is produced in St.-Emilion. Since the

65

growers of Burgundy know that they can easily sell whatever they produce, prices at the cellars have increased steadily in every good vintage. I recall a buying trip during which a grower in Pommard announced that he planned to increase his prices for the current vintage because hailstorms had reduced his crop.

"Last year it was frost. This year it's hail," I said jokingly. "What will it be next year?"

"Locusts," said the grower.

Despite the very high prices of the best Burgundy appellations, a substantial amount of wine made in Burgundy is entitled only to the appellation Bourgogne Rouge. For the most part this wine comes from lesser plots that are not entitled to individual village appellations, but Bourgogne Rouge is nevertheless made entirely from the Pinot Noir grape. Since Bourgogne Rouge is usually found on retail shelves for $3 to $3.75, it offers at least a taste of Burgundy at an affordable price. In general, this wine tends to be full and round, although naturally lacking the definition and distinct character of wines of a higher class. You can expect a decent wine with the characteristics of the Pinot Noir grape. In fact, a number of these wines are now labeled as Pinot Noir, to take advantage of the public's increasing awareness of the names of the best grape varieties. Bear in mind, however, that the *Appellation Contrôlée* will also appear on the label, and that this is your guide to just what the wine is. Remember also that in France, varietal labeling is generally used for lesser wines without glamorous appellations of their own. For example, a Bourgogne Rouge might be labeled as Pinot Noir, and a Bourgogne Blanc as Pinot Chardonnay, but no shipper will label, say, a Nuits St.-Georges or Meursault by anything less than its correct, and more expensive, appellation.

If you enjoy the style of Burgundy, then a Bourgogne Rouge or Pinot Noir is a wine to look for. For one thing, these wines have a distinct style that has not yet been matched anywhere else. The Pinot Noir grape is a difficult variety to cultivate, even in Burgundy, and such red wines as Assmannhauser in Germany and Dôle in Switzerland, made primarily from this grape, are not notably successful. In California as well, wines made from the Pinot Noir have not yet achieved the general level of excellence of those made from the Cabernet Sauvignon or the Pinot Chardonnay. Furthermore, the wines of Beaujolais, and especially those from such villages as Moulin-à-Vent and Fleurie, have increased so much in price that today a Bourgogne Rouge often costs less. Everyone must determine for himself whether he prefers the charm of a Gamay or the character of a Pinot Noir, but the latter does offer good value, comparatively speaking.

Bourgogne Rouge is almost always a shipper's blend, rather than one from an individual grower, but occasionally a grower makes more wine than he is legally permitted to from vineyards entitled to a village appellation, and the excess must be declassified and sold as Bourgogne Rouge. Such bottles do not often show up on a retail shelf, but you may sometimes find wine from a reputable grower so labeled. Such a wine may be a good value, but bear in mind that no grower will sell off his best barrels under the lower appellation.

Although Bourgogne Rouge may be the only appellation in Burgundy that falls more or less within our price limits, there are some other wines from this region that are worth noting. Despite their $4 to $6 price, they offer an alternative to $10 bottles. Some come from villages along the Côte d'Or that are relatively unfamiliar, but whose wines are now seen here: **Fixin, Auxey-Duresses,**

Monthélie, Pernand-Vergelesses, St. Romain, Santenay, and Savigny-les-Beaune. There are also the two regional wines of Burgundy, Côte de Nuits-Villages and Côte de Beaune-Villages, each of which is made up of wines from lesser villages in their respective sections of the Côte d'Or. These two wines are often well made and worth paying $1 more than for a Bourgogne Rouge. Givry and Mercurey, which come from the Côte Chalonnaise, south of the Côte de Beaune, are also becoming more widely available. All these wines tend to be somewhat lighter in style than those of the best-known Burgundy villages, but the best of them have a charm and elegance that is often lacking in the more commercial wines sold as Pommard and Nuits St.-Georges. Unfortunately, all of these appellations are available in fairly limited quantities—Savigny-les-Beaune, Mercurey, and Santenay are the most abundant—so that they are bound to increase steadily in price as they become better known.

An unusual and less familiar appellation from Burgundy is Bourgogne-Passe-Tout-Grains, made up of a mixture of the Pinot Noir (which must make up at least one-third of the blend) and the Gamay (which normally makes better wine farther south, in Beaujolais). Bourgogne-Passe-Tout-Grains is not often shipped here and is rarely featured on a label, but the appellation occasionally turns up in small print. The firm of Sichel, for example, markets a fresh and appealing wine under the varietal name Pinot Noir-Gamay, thereby featuring two well-known grape varieties for the price of one—the more expensive one.

The Mâcon region, which lies about halfway between Dijon and Lyon, produces both red and white wines. The reds are made from the Gamay grape, and therefore bear a slight resemblance to Beaujolais, although Mâcon lacks the fruit and charm of a good Beaujolais. Here again, some of the red wines from Mâcon are now labeled as **Gamay**. Generally speaking, the white wines of this region are more successful than the reds, which seem to me somewhat short in flavor and often not much more than an indistinct red wine. It is probably better to spend a little more and buy a Beaujolais instead.

Bourgueil
Chinon
Saumur-Champigny

These three wines from the Loire are made primarily from the Cabernet Franc grape (the Cabernet Sauvignon may also be used), and, not surprisingly, they exhibit the same distinct character found in red Bordeaux. At the same time, they are lighter-bodied, somewhat fruitier in style, and are sooner ready to drink. Almost all wines labeled Saumur are white, so this name was combined with that of the neighboring village of Champigny for red wines. Chinon and Bourgueil produce wines attractive enough to justify a search, but they are all bound to increase in price from $3 or less to $4 or more. Ackerman-Laurance Chinon and Wildman Bourgueil are two good examples.

Corbières
Minervois
Fitou

The Midi region in the south of France produces tremendous quantities of *vin ordinaire*. Within this vast region are a number of small districts whose wines are good enough to be sold with a VDQS appellation,* among them Corbières and Minervois. Fitou, less familiar here, is an *Appellation Contrôlée* wine. These wines are made from similar grape varieties as Côtes-du-Rhône, which they resemble in taste. Although these appellations are harder to find than is Côtes-du-Rhône, they are usually less expensive, and as such offer good value in red wine. The Corbières of Sichel is a case in point.

Côtes-du-Rhône

Châteauneuf-du-Pape is the best-known appellation of the Rhône Valley, and one of the most famous red wines of France. Its popularity is such that it has overshadowed the widely available regional appellation Côtes-du-Rhône, which accounts for more than ten times as much wine. Not only is Côtes-du-Rhône a better value than Châteauneuf-du-Pape, but it can occasionally be a better wine as well.

The hot climate typical of southern France precludes the use of the finest wine grapes along the Rhône. In fact, about a dozen varieties are permitted, since in a warm climate a combination of several grapes traditionally produces a better wine than any single variety used alone. Grenache and Carignan, the principal varieties cultivated, are also widely planted in the Midi region of France and in California's hot Central Valley, two regions better known for quantity than for quality. This is not to say that you cannot get a good bottle of wine from the Rhône, but only to point out the over-all limitations of these wines. At their best, Rhône wines can be described

---

* *Vins Délimités de Qualité Supérieure* is a legally defined category that includes about 50 wines that rank just below those of *Appellation Contrôlée* status.

as warm, full, and generous, rather than as wines with finesse or a distinct personality.

At $4 to $8, Châteauneuf-du-Pape is beyond our limits, and is something of an overpriced wine as well. On the other hand, there are too many examples of Côtes-du-Rhône shipped here for this appellation to be recommended without reservation. The lack of definition in Rhône wines is such that the abilities of each shipper count for more than the appellation of the wine. For example, it is not impossible to find a Côtes-du-Rhône that is better made than someone else's Châteauneuf-du-Pape, or to come across a Châteauneuf-du-Pape that is richer and better balanced than a more expensive Hermitage or Côte-Rôtie from the northern Rhône district. The obverse of this proposition is that a poor Côtes-du-Rhône can be a very uninteresting wine indeed, light and thin, and perhaps aging too fast. Côtes-du-Rhône varies in price from $1.50 to $3.50, the former of uncertain quality, the latter too expensive for this style of wine. Nevertheless, I would sooner take a chance on an unfamiliar Côtes-du-Rhône at $2 or less than on a Châteauneuf-du-Pape for much less than $5: a cheap Châteauneuf-du-Pape may turn out to be nothing more than an expensive Côtes-du-Rhône. Chapoutier, Delas, Rochette, and Jaboulet Aîné are dependable Rhône shippers; Château Malijay and La Vieille Ferme are both attractive examples of Côtes-du-Rhône.

ITALY

Barbera

The most famous wines of the Piedmont, in northern Italy, are labeled with the name of the village from which

each one comes—Barolo, Barbaresco, and Gattinara. At
$4 to $6 a bottle, these wines are well beyond our limits,
but there are other Piedmont wines available at half the
price that are not only better value, but often more appealing. Although Barolo is often referred to as the best
red wine of Italy, most examples are aged in wood for so
long that they exhibit a more-or-less dried-out taste that
is more highly prized by Italian connoisseurs than by
American wine drinkers. Barolo is often more impressive
than it is enjoyable.

In contrast, such wines as Barbera, Nebbiolo, and
Grignolino, each named after the grape variety from
which it is made, are usually fresher, bottled sooner to
retain more fruit, and generally more attractive. Barbera
is the most easily found, and the best examples are usually sold under the more specific *Denominazione di
Origine Controllata* Barbera d'Alba or Barbera d'Asti.
Grignolino is a lighter wine, with a fresh acidity that
gives it a slightly tart taste; **Nebbiolo** is somewhat fuller.
Bersano, Borgogno, Calissano, Fontanafredda, Giri and
Troglia are among the most dependable producers.

Chianti

There is probably no wine more famous than Chianti,
and no store is without a few examples, at prices ranging
from $1.50 for a straw-covered *fiasco* to $4.50 or more
for some of the best-known Riservas. There are so many
brands of Chianti available, at so many prices, that there
is bound to be a certain variation in style and quality, although not so much as in previous years. The new *Denominazione di Origine Controllata* laws have established
stricter controls on the wines from the Chianti region,

situated south of Florence in Tuscany, and consistent quality is available from a great many brands.

From a consumer's point of view, there are two basic distinctions to be made about Chianti. One is between wines in straw-covered *fiaschi* and those in regular Bordeaux-style bottles. The other, easily determined from the label but less easily defined in the wines themselves, is between those from the inner Chianti Classico zone and those from the rest of the region.

Chianti Classico accounts for only 20 percent or so of the total amount of Chianti produced, and a certain glamour has attached itself to this name. There are, in fact, six other delimited production zones within the Chianti region, but their names are not well known and rarely appear on a label. The neck seal to which the Classico wines are entitled is familiar to many consumers, however, and consists of the *gallo nero,* or black cockerel, on a gold ground within a red circle. There are, of course, a number of excellent Chianti Classico estates, of which Brolio is perhaps the most famous, but the seal is not in itself a guarantee of quality. For one thing, there are a surprising number of Chiantis sold here that bear the Classico seal, some of which are comparatively light and weak. For another, although the Classico zone is delimited, a producer can use up to 15 percent of wines from outside the zone and still use the Classico appellation. In short, the name of the producer is finally more important than the appearance of the *gallo nero:* Ruffino and Frescobaldi, for example, make good Chianti that does not carry the Classico seal.

The difference between Chianti sold in *fiaschi* and in straight-sided bottles is more easily defined. Although the cost of labor is now such that a *fiasco* is more expensive to produce than a regular bottle, the wine in the

73

fiasco is generally less good. Since *fiaschi* are hard to
store on their sides, and the corks used for them fairly
short, the wines they contain are not meant to age, and
should not be kept for any length of time. If you compare
several wines shipped in *fiaschi* and in bottles, you will
discover that the former are lighter, younger wines, the
latter bigger, fuller, and longer-lived. This rule of thumb
concerning quality is, however, complicated by price.
Most *fiaschi* hold 32 ounces, bottles only 24 ounces, so
that a *fiasco* that sells for $2 is the equivalent of a bottle
at $1.50. In effect, an inexpensive *fiasco* of Chianti is
among the least expensive red wines.

Just how much of a value inexpensive Chianti is depends on your attitude toward this wine. There is no
question that certain Chiantis that sell for $3 to $4 a bottle, such as Brolio Riserva, Nozzole, Straccali Riserva, and
Serristori Macchiavelli, are better than those available for
$1.50 to $2.50 a *fiasco*. Riservas, in particular, which
have to be at least three years old, are pretty dependable.
They are rarely fine wines, however, and there is something of a limit to how good Chianti can be. Subtlety,
elegance, and a distinct taste are not its principal characteristics, and often enough older Chiantis lack fruit and
charm. The difference in quality between a $2 Chianti
and one priced at $4 is rarely as big as the difference in
price, especially if the less expensive wine comes in a
quart *fiasco*. If you accept the light-bodied and occasionally mildly raisiny quality found in many Italian
wines, inexpensive Chianti becomes one of the most
easily available wine values. Note that a *fiasco* is not always the best value from a specific producer. If his
Chianti Classico Riserva is $3.75 and his *fiasco* is $3, the
comparative value is obvious, but if the bottle is $2.95
and the *fiasco* $3.75, the bottle, which contains the bet-

ter wine, is easily the better value. You will want to try some of the inexpensive *fiaschi* available locally, but brands in general distribution that sell for $2.50 or less include Barsottini, Bigi, Bucalossi, Giannozzi, Cimamori Pagni, and Soderi. Brolio, Melini, and Ruffino ship dependable wines in *fiaschi*, but they cost about $1 more.

Lambrusco

Two or three years ago, Lambrusco was practically unknown here; today it is the most popular red wine of Italy after Chianti. Lambrusco, named after the grape from which it is made, is unusual among red wines because it is more or less sweet and because it retains a very slight sparkle that shows up as a pink foam when the wine is first poured out. The sudden success of this light, fruity wine undoubtedly owes much to the fact that it is semi-sweet, slightly sparkling, and costs $2.50 or less. Although Lambrusco has made its name here as a sweet, fizzy wine for people who don't like wine, there is a certain variation in style to be found, depending on the shipper and the demands of his American importer. Lambrusco has always been considered an excellent accompaniment to the rich foods of its native Bologna, and you may be happily surprised if you try such full-flavored and comparatively dry examples as those from Riunite, Calissano, and Fabiano.

Valpolicella
Bardolino

The district of Valpolicella and the village of Bardolino produce comparatively light-bodied, enjoyable wines that are widely available in stores and restaurants. Bardolino is much the lighter of the two, and generally much less interesting as a wine. Valpolicella ranges in price from $1.50 or less for private labels and minor brands to $3.25 or so for such popular brands as Bertani, Bolla, and Ruffino. Although Valpolicella is obviously not one of the best values in red wines, cheaper examples—with the exception of Ricasoli—will almost always prove disappointing, even if judged simply as red wine.

Valpolicella is best drunk young, but it may be difficult to figure out which are the youngest wines available. The vintages indicated on the labels of the major brands at any given time may span five years, although it is unlikely that there is that much difference in the ages of the wines themselves.

Valtellina
Inferno
Grumello
Sassella

The terraced vineyards of the Valtellina Valley in northern Italy produce attractive $3 wines which are starting to appear here, although they are not yet easy to find. The official appellation is Valtellina or Valtellina Superiore, but the name of one or another of the small inner districts—Inferno, Grumello and Sassella—is usually displayed more prominently on the label. The wines are made primarily from the Nebbiolo grape, widely cultivated in the Piedmont, but Valtellina wines are lighter and softer than, for example, a Barolo. Orfevi, Nino Negri, and Pelizzati ship Valtellina wines here.

RED WINES

SPAIN

Rioja

There are hundreds of vineyards in Bordeaux whose names are unfamiliar to most consumers, and which are collectively referred to as *petits châteaux*. I once asked a Bordeaux shipper whether the proper translation of *petits châteaux* should be "lesser châteaux," rather than the more literal "small châteaux," since many of these properties were actually quite large.

"Oh, yes," he agreed. "Many of them are very big indeed. In fact, some of them extend all the way into Spain."

Although the Bordelais have always known about the wines of Rioja, 120 miles away, most American consumers are more familiar with fruit-flavored Sangria. Nevertheless, a surprising number of wines from Rioja are now being shipped to this country, and since many of them sell for less than $2.50 a bottle, they include some of the very best values among well-made red wines.

Rioja is a specific district appellation in Spain, and every bottle bears on its label a small design resembling a postage stamp with the word Rioja on it. Many bottles also carry a back label with a colorful map of the Rioja district, more or less in the shape of a bull. Although other Spanish wines are becoming available here—such as those of La Mancha and Valdepeñas, and the Catalonian wines from villages near Barcelona—none of these wines has the style or distinction of Rioja, which is the best red-wine-producing district in Spain.

The wines of Rioja are known by the name of the producing winery coupled with an imaginative proprietary

77

name—such as Viña Pomal, Banda Azul, Cepa de Oro, or Monte Real—rather than by vineyard or village appellations, as in France and Germany, or by grape variety, as in California. Each shipper actually markets several styles of Rioja and identifies each one by labeling it with a different brand name. A typical selection would include a young red wine, a moderately aged one, and a specially selected older red wine with several years in wood; among the whites, a light dry wine, perhaps a fuller-bodied one, and a semisweet wine. Whereas in the cellars of Bordeaux or Burgundy a visitor is traditionally offered the opportunity to taste wines still in wood, a visitor to a Rioja *bodega,* or cellar, will invariably be offered bottled wines, as would be the case in a Champagne house. In other words, the wines in barrel do not represent individual vineyards or appellations at an early stage of their development, but rather the basic materials from which the shipper's different brands will be blended. Consequently, tasting wines in wood in a Rioja cellar won't give you much idea of what you'll be getting in bottle. On the other hand, this blending of various wines results in a continuity of style among the different grades, and given the low prices at which Rioja is sold, this continuity may be of greater value to a consumer than the more complex and less certain pleasure of following the development of the wine of a specific vineyard in a particular vintage.

A few wines from Rioja are still labeled as Chablis or Burgundy, rather than with a proprietary name. The use of these generic names is gradually disappearing, and is not often used by the top producers, who prefer, naturally enough, to feature the names that they have created.

Vintages usually don't mean a great deal on Rioja labels, except as an indication of the relative age within the range of wines offered by a single firm. Thus, the least expensive wines currently on the market from three shippers might be labeled 1961, 1966, and 1969 respectively, yet each wine is probably a blend of two- or three-year-old wines.

A vintage year may be preceded by the word *Vendimia* or *Cosecha*, which means vintage or harvest, but a more important word is *Reserva*. Among the wines maturing in a shipper's cellars are some which he feels have the depth of character that would enable them to benefit from additional aging, and these older, specially selected wines are eventually marketed as Reservas. It is an important characteristic of all but the very cheapest Riojas that they are aged in wood longer than most of the world's red wines, and are thus more mature when they appear on the market. The best of these wines are the Reservas, many of which are ten years old or more. What makes them exceptionally interesting—and well worth seeking out—is their price. Some Reservas are comparatively light and soft, such as La Rioja Alta's Reserva 904, Bodegas Bilbainas' Vendimia Especial and Cune's Imperial Reserva. Other examples are fuller and richer, including the Castillo Ygay Reservas of the Marqués de Murrieta and Bodegas Bilbainas' Viña Pomal Reserva.

Most of the red wines of Rioja are dependable and well-priced, but they do have certain limiting characteristics. Since they are made from a mixture of several grapes, including the Grenache—as is the case with Rhône wines—they lack the definition and distinct personality of, say, a Bordeaux, with its Cabernet Sauvignon base. The least expensive vary in style from those with a forthright freshness to some that are rather light and very slightly sharp. They can be good value, however, and if they lack the flavor and maturity that can make Rioja such a good wine, they nevertheless have a youthful freshness and appeal that is not often found in such inexpensive wines. At the other end of the spectrum, some of the older wines have a pronounced woody character, especially admired by the people who made them, but not so attractive to palates less used to this slightly oxidized style. At present, the middle range of wines—$1.75 to $3.50—is the most successful, combining good flavor with some style, and maturity without an excessively woody taste.

The following list, although not meant to be complete, lists about 25 red wines from Rioja. The wines marketed by each firm are in ascending order of price and thus reflect the quality as determined by the shipper, usually as a function of the wine's age. Naturally, younger and cheaper wines may be better values. Note that the same proprietary name may be used both for a current vintage and for a Reserva. For example, Cune (as this firm is generally referred to) markets their Viña Real both as a young wine and as a Reserva Especial, and Bodegas Bilbainas' Viña Pomal is obtainable with a recent vintage and also as a Reserva Especial. The Reserva will bear a vintage ten or fifteen years older than that on the current wine. Whether or not the dates are accurate, the Reserva will almost always exhibit considerably more depth and richness of flavor.

Bodegas Bilbainas	Rioja Itzarra
	Viña Pomal
	Viña Zaco
	Vendimia Especial
	Viña Pomal Reserva
Bodegas Franco-Españolas	Rioja
	Claret

Bodegas Gomez Cruzado	Rioja
Bodegas Riojanas	Monte Real
Bodegas Unidas	AGE
	Siglo
Compania Vinicola del Norte de España (Cune)	Clarete Cune
	Viña Real
	Imperial
	Viña Real Reserva
	Imperial Gran Reserva
Federico Paternina	Banda Azul
	Viña Vial
	Gran Reserva
La Rioja Alta	Viña Ardanza
	Reserva "904"
Lopez de Heredia	Viña Tondonia
	Viña Bosconia
	Viña Tondonia Reserva
Marqués de Murrieta	Rioja
Marqués de Riscal	Rioja
Rioja Santiago	Yago

Although Rioja is the best red wine of Spain, wines from other parts of the country are becoming popular here as well. The **La Mancha** district, which contains the village of **Valdepeñas**, produces wines that are fresh, light, and appealing when they are young—reminiscent of Beaujolais and much less expensive. Castillo de Mudela is a good example.

Catalonia, with Barcelona as its principal city, produces agreeable red wines that are available for $2.50 or less. The Tinto of Rene Barbier and Coronas of Miguel Torres are two widely distributed Catalonian wines.

Other inexpensive Spanish wines without specific appellations include Bon-Sol Rojo Montaña and such brands as Marqués de Iberica, Juan Hernandez, and Avallon.

PORTUGAL

Dao

The region of Dão, in north central Portugal, produces a substantial amount of red and white wine, and a number of examples are now available here at $2.25 to $3. The style of red Dão has been described as being halfway between a Bordeaux and a Burgundy, which accurately suggests a wine of some character that is nevertheless round rather than tannic. The best selling Dão is Grão Vasco, a well-made wine which is more widely distributed than is usually the case with wines from unfamiliar regions: it is shipped by the same firm that produces Mateus Rosé. Other good examples are Real Vinicola Dão Cabido and Borlidos Dão S. Vicente.

Almost all of the wines shipped from Portugal are rosés, so Dão is almost the only red wine that can be found. The Vinho Verde district, known here for its white wines, also produces red wines that are tart, acid, and comparatively raw in style. They are unusual in that they are served cold, and also because they frequently accompany fish dishes. Red Vinho Verde is something of an acquired taste, as is the local codfish with which it is often served.

YUGOSLAVIA

Cabernet from Istria
Prokupac from Yovac
Plavac from Bol

For many years Yugoslavia has shipped a variety of inexpensive wines to this country, some of them selling for $1 a bottle and overpriced at that. Recently several of the largest producers wisely agreed to limit their shipments to the United States to a selection of their best wines, market them under a single brand name, Adriatica, and to label each wine with the name of the grape and the place of origin. In addition, the two biggest wineries continue to sell a few wines under their own brands, which are Slovin and Navip. All three are imported by a single American company, and altogether about two dozen red, white, and rosé wines are now available. Some of the varietal names and most of the wine districts are unfamiliar to American consumers, but they are worth some attention because Yugoslavia now offers some very attractive wines for $2.50 or less.

The red wines are fresh, distinct, and with the kind of character typical of young Bordeaux, whether or not they are made from the Cabernet. Prokupac and Plavac (pronounced prokupats and plavats) are native Yugoslavian grape varieties. The wines listed above are sold under the Adriatica label. The Slovin line also includes a Cabernet from Istria, and there is a Prokupac from Vranje and a Gamay from Vencac sold under the Navip label.

HUNGARY

Egri Bikavér
Szeksárdi Vörös

Hungarian wine labels can be discouraging until you understand that the first word is usually the place of origin. Just as German wine villages take on an -er ending on a label, so Hungarian place names take on an -i—the two red wines above come from Eger and Szeksárd. A factor that makes it easier to deal with these unusually named wines is that they are all shipped by Monimpex, the state export monopoly, so that there are only a limited number of Hungarian wines available here.

Egri Bikavér is the best known and most widely available of the red and white table wines. It is a full-bodied, somewhat tannic wine similar in style to a young Bordeaux. Szeksárdi Vörös is a better-balanced wine with more character, and it costs $1 less than Egri Bikavér. **Villányi Burgundi** is another attractive wine that is now available in this country.

GREECE

Red Wine

The appeal of Greek red wines is that they are dependable, distinct, and cost $2 to $2.50. On the other hand, there are other full-flavored red wines to be found for the same price that are less aggressive in taste. If you try one of these wines when you eat in a Greek restaurant, you will find that its strong, tart flavor complements the oil-based dishes of that country. You may therefore want to drink a Greek red wine occasionally when you serve rich food, cooling the bottle as is generally done in restaurants.

Finding a good example of Greek wine is easy. Only a few shippers are widely represented, and each one sells one or two wines labeled with a proprietary name rather than a regional appellation. The best known include Demestica and Castel Danielis of Achaia, Clauss; Pendeli of Cambas; and Mont Ambelos of Nicolaou.

CHILE

Cabernet Sauvignon
Burgundy

Only a few Chilean wines are available here, but they are well worth looking for, since they are among the best values to be found among red wines for $2 or less. In the middle of the nineteenth century, Chilean landowners brought in French wine experts, many of them from Bordeaux, to develop their vineyards. As a result, there is a great deal of acreage planted in such Bordeaux varieties as Cabernet Sauvignon, Cabernet Franc, Merlot, Sauvignon Blanc and Sémillon—more than in California, surprisingly enough. Chilean wines are shipped in the squat *Bocksbeutel* and in Bordeaux bottles, and they are marketed both as varietal wines—Cabernet, Pinot, Reisling—and with such generic names as Burgundy and Rhine wine. The wines sold as Cabernet or Cabernet Sauvignon are the best; they have a more distinct varietal character than the softer, agreeable wines sold as Pinot or Pinot Noir. In fact, there is not much Pinot Noir

85

planted in Chile. The white wines of Chile are less of a value than the reds.

The two best-known brands and their red wines are:

Concha y Toro:	Cabernet Sauvignon
	Pinot Noir
	Burgundy
Undurraga:	Cabernet Reservado
	Pinot

UNITED STATES

CALIFORNIA:

Burgundy
Claret
Chianti
Mountain Red

California table wines are often divided into two basic categories—generic wines, such as Chablis, Burgundy, and Chianti, which take their names from existing European wine districts; and varietal wines, such as Cabernet Sauvignon, Chenin Blanc, and Pinot Noir, named after the grape variety from which each one is primarily made. Most wineries market both generic and varietal wines, and the difference between the two is sometimes easier to recognize on the label than in the wine. There are generically labeled wines with distinct characteristics, and varietal wines lacking a definable personality. However, as almost all California wines are labeled generically or varietally, it seems logical to divide them accordingly.

California generic wines account for most of the table wine sold in the United States. Many brands are marketed in gallons and half-gallons, and they are among the most easily found and least expensive of the world's wines available in this country. Besides generic appellations, a few wineries, including Almadén, Beringer/Los Hermanos, Korbel, Martini, and Sebastiani, also market a less expensive line of Mountain wines, sold simply as Mountain White and Mountain Red, or as Mountain White Chablis, Mountain Red Burgundy, and so on. Inglenook sells some of its generic wines as North Coast Counties Vintage Wines, and its less expensive generics under the Navalle label.

When buying generic wines, you should remember that they have more in common with each other than with the wines whose names are being used. These few names represent, in effect, nonvarietal wines which are relatively inexpensive and in abundant supply. It is perverse to insist that a particular California Chablis or Burgundy does not taste like the original French example. Ignoring differences of soil and climate, the wines would have to be made from the Pinot Chardonnay and Pinot Noir grapes respectively, and no California producer is going to market wines made from such expensive grapes as inexpensive generics. The problem with generic wines is not that they don't taste like the European originals, but that there are no consistent standards that help the consumer find his way from one brand to another. Perhaps the most important difference between different generic wines, especially to anyone used to European wines, is that some are dry and some are not. While a certain amount of sweetness in both white and red wines appeals to a large segment of the public, those who prefer completely dry table wines cannot simply assume that a Chablis will be drier than a Sauterne, or a Claret drier than a Burgundy. For one thing, some wineries market identical wines under different generic labels. For another, many wineries maintain a minimum amount of sweetness in all their wines, others in none of them. The amount of measurable sugar present in a Chablis or Burgundy may be as much as 2 percent, which is far from dry.

As a rule of thumb, generic wines sold in bottles with screw tops are likely to be somewhat sweeter than those in corked bottles. Also, both red and white wines with Italian names, such as Fortissimo, Paisano, and Vino da Tavola, are usually sweet, and are often described as "mellow" on the label.

The other basic difference among generic wines concerns the style of winemaking, although this is harder to define than is the amount of sweetness present. Put in simple terms, there are at one end the wineries who produce agreeable wines, comparatively neutral in character, without any aging or particular style. At the other end are those wineries whose generic wines have a recognizable character and whose wines have been aged, sometimes even in small barrels, to achieve some depth of flavor and even a complexity of taste. Beaulieu Vineyard Burgundy, Christian Brothers Claret, Charles Krug Claret and Burgundy, Paul Masson Burgundy, Martini Claret and Mirassou Burgundy are some of the generic wines in the second category. If they are not the least expensive generics, these wines are nevertheless more interesting than the names Burgundy or Claret would suggest.

Although most California wines are marketed under either a generic or varietal name, a few wineries have created proprietary names for certain of their wines. For example, Paul Masson sells two red wines called Rubion and Baroque, and two whites called Rhine Castle and Emerald Dry. Chateau La Salle is a sweet white wine marketed by The Christian Brothers, and Barenblut is a red from Beringer/Los Hermanos. At a lower price level, Charles Krug markets Bravissimo and Fortissimo under its inexpensive CK Mondavi label, Vino da Tavola is produced by Guild, and Gallo labels one of its popular red wines Paisano.

California wines have traditionally been divided into two price groups—the premium wines and those referred to as bulk wines. The second category includes such wines as Gallo, Italian Swiss Colony, and others which retail for $1 to $1.50 a bottle, $3 to $5.50 a gallon. Almadén, Paul Masson, and The Christian Brothers are the best known and most widely available brands among premium wines. Most premium generic wines sell for $1.75 to $2.50 a bottle, $6 to $8 a gallon.

The list below includes a selection of generic wines that have been divided into the two traditional price groups. While the separation may be useful to those involved in the marketing of these wines, it is less valid for the consumer. Some of the least expensive wines are as well made as those that cost $1 or $2 more a gallon, and offer especially good value. The inexpensive wines listed in the first group are characterized by a grapey berrylike flavor, however, and they are generally sweeter than the more expensive generics. Among them, Gallo Hearty Burgundy seems to have the most body and flavor, CK Mondavi Burgundy is the driest, and Gallo Burgundy and Winemaster's Guild Burgundy are the lightest-bodied.

CK Mondavi	Burgundy
Gallo	Burgundy
	Hearty Burgundy
Guild	Tavola Red
	Winemaster's Guild Burgundy

Italian Swiss Colony	Burgundy Napa-Sonoma- Mendocino Burgundy
Beaulieu Vineyard	Burgundy
Christian Brothers	Claret
Charles Krug	Burgundy Claret
Korbel	Burgundy
Martini	Mountain Red Mountain Claret
Paul Masson	Burgundy Baroque
Mirassou	Burgundy

CALIFORNIA:

Cabernet Sauvignon
Zinfandel
Gamay
Gamay Beaujolais

From the beginning of commercial production, California wines have been labeled with such European place names as Chablis, Burgundy, and Chianti. Occasionally a winery would market one of its wines with the name of the grape variety from which it was made, but as consumers were not yet familiar with these names, varietal labeling, as this is called, was slow to get started. Fifteen years ago it was still easier for a producer to sell a wine made from Cabernet Sauvignon as Claret, rather than as a varietal. Today the situation is completely reversed. As winemakers continue to discover the best vineyard sites for each of the top varieties, and as consumers realize that many varietal wines represent the best that California has to offer, varietal labeling has caught on to such an extent that there are now two dozen red and white varietal wines marketed under their own names. Most of these grape varieties are associated with specific wine regions of Europe, and include Cabernet Sauvignon from Bordeaux; Pinot Noir, Gamay, and Gamay Beaujolais from Burgundy; Petite Sirah from the Rhône Valley; Barbera from northern Italy; and Zinfandel, whose exact European place of origin is not certain.

Other varietals, each of which is associated with a particular winery, include Pinot St. George of The Christian Brothers, Charbono of Inglenook, and Grignolino of Heitz. Most varietals, however, are available from many wineries, so that there are several hundred individual varietal wines produced in California today.

Almost all of the popular varietal wines come from the North Coast counties that fan out from San Francisco —Sonoma, Mendocino, Napa, Alameda (which includes the Livermore Valley), Santa Clara, San Benito, and Monterey. If at least 75 percent of the grapes used to make a specific wine come from one of these counties, its name may appear on the label. In addition, some wineries are now labeling their wines with the words "North Coast Counties." Geographical appellations have never played the same role in California as they do in Europe, so that the varietal name is usually as much as you are told about the wine in the bottle. Nevertheless, the differences between wines with the same name can be enormous, both in quality and in price. This stems from the fact that a California winemaker has much more flexibility in making his wines than his European counterpart. A

European winemaker is to a large extent bound within established norms: the limits of the vineyard or estate have long been defined, the grapes he may use are regulated by law, and the winemaking techniques are traditional.

In contrast, a California winemaker can choose the site on which to establish a new vineyard or the region from which he will buy grapes. He can choose the varieties from which he will produce wines, deciding whether to limit himself to two or three wines or to market a complete line. If he makes generic wines, he decides which grapes will go into his Burgundy or Chablis. If he makes varietal wines, he can determine how much more than 51 percent—the legal minimum—he will use of any given variety. Vinification, aging, and treatment of wines varies from one winemaker to another throughout the world, but there are perhaps more options available to the California winemaker. To take one example, two distinct wines are made from the Sauvignon Blanc grape. One is a semisweet wine similar to a light Sauternes, the other is a crisp, dry wine similar to a Sancerre, and sometimes sold as Fumé Blanc. Some wineries prefer to make rounded, appealing red wines by aging them in giant redwood vats; others use small oak barrels, as in Bordeaux and Burgundy, to add complexity and longevity to their wines. Wines are usually fined, or clarified, before being bottled to remove any impurities, but fining may also strip a wine of some of its character. Some wineries use heavy fining to produce brilliant wines, others do not fine at all, in order to retain more depth and richness of flavor in certain red wines.

The many approaches to winemaking that are possible in California, combined with the skills and intent of each winery, result in a much greater variation among different wines with the same generic or varietal name than the label might lead you to expect. This explains why it is possible to find Zinfandel from $1 to $5 a bottle, and Cabernet Sauvignon or Pinot Chardonnay from $3 to $10. High prices are always to some extent the result of scarcity, but quality plays an even more important role.

Variations of quality exist not only from one winery to another, but from one varietal appellation to another. Despite their popularity, some grape varieties do not usually produce very interesting wines, and therefore cannot be considered good value. The most consistently successful red varietal wines are Cabernet Sauvignon and Zinfandel. Although most examples of Cabernet Sauvignon are priced beyond our limits, even less expensive brands, which may lack the varietal character and definition of the best bottles, nevertheless include some well-made and distinct wines. Zinfandel has always been extensively planted throughout the state, and it makes a fresh, spicy, and distinct wine that has traditionally been used in generic Burgundy and Claret. Now accepted on its own as a varietal, it is sometimes vinified and aged to produce a tannic, full-flavored wine reminiscent of Cabernet Sauvignon, but more often it is made into a fresh, spicy, young wine that resembles Beaujolais.

There has been some uncertainty as to whether it is the Gamay or the Gamay Beaujolais, both of which are planted in California, that is the true grape of France's Beaujolais district. It may be that the Gamay Beaujolais—despite its name—is actually related to the Pinot Noir. More to the point, the wines made in California from these two varieties sometimes lack the fruit and charm of Beaujolais, and the distinction of Zinfandel, although a few well-made wines are available. The Petite Sirah, also widely used for generic red wines, is increasingly seen as a varietal, albeit not a very distinguished one. Despite its reputation and its high price, the Pinot Noir has not yet achieved the same general level of success in California as the Cabernet Sauvignon. It is widely available, but most examples are comparatively light-bodied, lack varietal character, and are not a dependable value.

The wines listed below do not represent the best varietal wines of California, but rather a selection of well-made wines that are generally available throughout the country for $2.50 to $3.50 or so. Just as the top vineyards of Bordeaux, Burgundy, and the Rhine are not included in this guide, so many excellent wines from small and medium-sized wineries have been left out for reasons of price or availability. Prices for California varietal wines have increased steadily, along with those of the most popular imported wines. If California wines continue to increase in price while inexpensive wines from less familiar regions of the world become more widely available, some of the wines listed below will become less of a value than they are now. Nevertheless, this list should serve as a guide to some of the more interesting California wines in general distribution.

Almadén	Zinfandel
Beaulieu Vineyard	Gamay Beaujolais
Beringer	Zinfandel
Buena Vista	Zinfandel
Christian Brothers	Cabernet Sauvignon
	Gamay Noir
	Zinfandel
Inglenook	Zinfandel
	Gamay Beaujolais
Charles Krug	Zinfandel

Louis Martini	Cabernet Sauvignon
	Barbera
	Zinfandel
Paul Masson	Gamay Beaujolais
	Cabernet Sauvignon
Robert Mondavi	Gamay
Sebastiani	Zinfandel

NEW YORK STATE:

Burgundy
Claret
Red Wine

The most popular New York State wines have such a unique taste that it is difficult to place them in the context of the wines of the world. Most of them are characterized by a grapey, pungent flavor typical of the native American grape varieties from which so many of these wines are made. This taste is not unattractive, but it is different enough to surprise anyone not prepared for it. Perhaps even more important, almost all of the widely available red, white, and pink New York State wines are sweet, and a few of them are among the sweetest wines in the world. It is probable that anyone who drinks these wines regularly would find Beaujolais, Chianti, Pouilly-Fuissé, or California Chablis much too dry. Conversely, a wine drinker opening his first bottle of New York State red or white wine might find it both too sweet and too unusual.

Difficult as these wines are to categorize, they are nevertheless well-made, appealing, and not expensive: most examples sell for $1.75 to $2.25, some for even less.

Four brands—Widmer, Taylor, Great Western, and Gold Seal—dominate the market for New York State wines, and their wines are widely available. Generically labeled New York State wines include Burgundy, Claret, Chablis, Sauterne, and Rhine Wine; varietal wines are made from such native American grapes as Concord, Catawba, Niagara, Isabella, Delaware, Duchess, and Moore's Diamond. Proprietary names have been used with great success for New York State wines, either by themselves, or in combination with varietal names: Lake Country Red, Naples Valley Red, Pleasant Valley Red, Pleasant Valley Pink Catawba, Lake Niagara, Lake Roselle, and so on.

Attractive examples of New York State red wines—semisweet and distinctive in taste—include Gold Seal Catawba Red, Great Western Pleasant Valley Red, Taylor Lake Country Red and Claret, and Widmer Naples Valley Red.

There is a second category of New York State wines, produced in increasing quantities, which are made from French-American hybrids. Wines made from hybrids, which are a genetic cross between native and American grape varieties, do not exhibit the grapey flavor usually associated with New York State wines. They may lack a definite personality of their own, but they are attractive and inexpensive dry red wines. Chelois and Baco Noir are the names of two of these hybrids, and they are marketed as such by Great Western. Boordy Vineyards Red Wine and the more expensive Bully Hill Red Wine are two more good examples.

White Wines

FRANCE

Alsatian Riesling
Alsatian Sylvaner

Although Alsace produces more white wine of good quality than any other region of France except Bordeaux, its wines have yet to become popular here. One reason is that—confusingly enough—these French wines are shipped in tapering German wine bottles, and are labeled with grape names associated with German wines. In fact, except for Muscadet, Alsace is the only *Appellation Contrôlée* region of France whose wines are labeled with the name of the grape from which they are made—Sylvaner, Riesling, Gewürztraminer, Pinot Blanc, Tokay d'Alsace—rather than with a precise geographical place of origin. The Gewürztraminer is so unusual that it is described at length elsewhere; Pinot Blanc and Tokay d'Alsace (which is the Pinot Gris) are rarely shipped here.

Although Alsatian wines used to be referred to, correctly, as French Rhine wines, they are quite different in style from those of Germany. Alsace produces fairly full-flavored white wines that retain the style of the Sylvaner and Riesling, but without being sweet; and they do not have the delicate floweriness of German wines. The Sylvaner produces a comparatively neutral wine, but with a certain amount of fresh acidity and crispness of taste. By comparison, California Riesling, which is in fact made from the Sylvaner, tends to be somewhat less crisp and slightly more expensive than Alsatian Sylvaner, which costs about $2.75. Most Alsatian shippers price their Riesling at $1 more than their Sylvaner, and correctly so—it is a dry wine with more flavor and a more distinct personality. Nevertheless, the Sylvaner may be a better value, not so much in comparison to the Riesling, but in comparison to dry white wines from all over the world that are fairly bland and lack its refreshing acidity.

There are no districts within Alsace whose names appear on a label, and very few wines come from a single vineyard. Alsatian wines are labeled, as are California varietal wines, simply with the name of the shipper and that of the grape. Alsatian shippers whose wines are generally available here include Hugel, Trimbach, Lorentz, Dopff, Dopff & Irion, and Willm, whose Cordon d'Alsace is a good value.

Gewürztraminer is associated with Alsace, and all of the Alsatian shippers market a Gewürztraminer along with a Sylvaner and Riesling. The wine made from this grape is so distinct, however, and so unlike any other wine in the world, that it deserves to be described separately. Gewürztraminer has a spicy, pungent bouquet and taste that are as unmistakable as that of, say, the Muscat grape. The wine is full-bodied and usually dry, although some shippers produce a slightly mellow Gewürz-traminer. The wine is so distinct that some people are put off by it, but it is unusual enough to try at least once; if you enjoy it you will have found a most interesting wine to serve.

The wine is actually made from the Traminer grape. The finished wine is then tasted, and the most typical and pungent lots have traditionally been marketed as Gewürztraminer (*gewürz* means spicy), the rest as Traminer. The Alsatian shippers agreed, however, that as of 1973 Traminer would no longer be a separate appellation —all the wines from this grape are now sold as Gewürztraminer. Most Gewürztraminers cost $3.50 to $4.50, so these wines are not inexpensive, but they are different enough so that those who enjoy this taste may find the extra cost worth it.

Although the Traminer is said to have originated in northern Italy, the only other wine region that produces this wine commercially—except for the Yugoslavian Traminec from Radgona—is California, where the wine is sold both as Gewürztraminer and as Traminer. Good examples are listed in the California section on page 128.

Bordeaux Blanc
Graves

More than half of the tremendous amount of *Appellation Contrôlée* wines produced in Bordeaux is white. About two-thirds of this is entitled only to the appellation Bordeaux Blanc, the rest to a dozen or so minor appellations that are not frequently seen here. Ignoring for the moment the sweet wines of Sauternes and Barsac— which are discussed elsewhere—the most famous white wine district of Bordeaux is Graves. Many consumers consider Graves and white Bordeaux to be virtually synonymous, and every Bordeaux shipper includes an example of this wine among his offering of Bordeaux appellations. Most shippers also market a Bordeaux Blanc, but not necessarily under that name.

Despite their fame and wide distribution, the dry white wines of Bordeaux have never been considered wines of particular class or style. Made primarily from the Sauvignon Blanc and Sémillon grapes, many of them lack the acidity that would give them a fresh and lively taste. Furthermore, because many Bordeaux Blanc and Graves are not altogether dry, their bouquet and taste are occasionally marred by the sulfur dioxide that is used to stabilize them. Other wine areas, notably California and Germany, have found ways to stabilize semidry white wines without an excessive use of sulfur, but the practice persists in Bordeaux. Despite these caveats, however, white Bordeaux has the advantage of being a comparative full-flavored and distinct wine that is widely available from a great many shippers. Chosen selectively, there are some values to be found here from $2 to $3.50.

Although Bordeaux Blanc is the basic appellation of this region, those words do not always dominate a label. Many shippers market a Bordeaux or Bordeaux Supérieur (the latter contains an extra degree of alcohol), but some call their wine Sauvignon Blanc or Sauvignon Sec, and others use a proprietary name such as Prince Blanc, Monopole, or Mouton Cadet. If a shipper creates a special name for a white Bordeaux, he will almost invariably use it for his Bordeaux Blanc rather than his Graves. As a result, there are many shippers whose Bordeaux Blanc—under whatever guise—turns out to be more expensive than their Graves, which is a higher appellation. Even when a shipper sells both wines under their respective appellations, the Graves is often about the same price as the Bordeaux Blanc, or only a little more. Consequently, Graves is often a better value, and, frequently enough, actually costs less than many Bordeaux Blancs.

The wines sold as Graves are a fairly dependable group, if you accept the basic character of white Bordeaux. Since there is something of a limit to how good white Graves can be, some of the more expensive château-bottled wines from this district are not noticeably better than the best of the regional wines. In fact, a few are less good, in that they display off-tastes that are not present in the shippers' blends.

Although there is good reason for choosing Graves over Bordeaux Blanc as a general rule, it will nevertheless pay you to experiment with white Bordeaux for under $2.50: you are likely to discover a decent enough private label or small château. **Entre-Deux-Mers** is a less familiar white Bordeaux appellation which is being shipped here in increasing quantities. Both regional wines and small châteaux can be found from this district, which produces more white wine than does Graves.

Here is a selection of well-made Bordeaux Blanc and Graves that are in general distribution. Most of them are fairly dry, although mild and round rather than crisp. The mellower wines, which are especially attractive if you enjoy wines that are not altogether dry, are indicated with an *.

Cordier	Graves
Cruse	Graves
	Château Lavie* (Bordeaux)
de Luze	Graves Royal
Ginestet	Sauvignon Blanc (Bordeaux)

Nathaniel Johnston	Graves*
Lavergne	Graves
Schröder & Schÿler	Château Malleprat* (Graves)
Sichel	Blanc de Blancs Sauvignon Sec (Bordeaux Blanc)
	Graves Bonne Terre*

Bourgogne Blanc
Mâcon Blanc
Pinot Chardonnay

The white wines of Burgundy are among the finest and most famous in the world. Many of these wines are now among the most expensive as well, although there are a few appellations that are still available for $4 or less. The most popular white Burgundies are Pouilly-Fuissé and Chablis. Pouilly-Fuissé has always been an agreeable, if undistinguished, wine; incredibly, it now sells regularly for $5 or more, with some bottles priced at $6 and $7. Chablis, although at its best a finer wine, sells for only a little less: many brands of Chablis and Chablis Premier Cru are now $4.50 to $6, and Chablis Grand Cru is often $6 or $7. As a result of the tremendous demand for these two wines, the classic white Burgundies from the villages of Meursault, Chassagne-Montrachet, and Puligny-Montrachet often cost no more, and sometimes less, than Pouilly-Fuissé or Chablis. These village wines are not inexpensive, of course, but they are usually better value.

If the only problem with white Burgundy were that it has increased in price, it would be discouraging enough. Unfortunately, as the price has gone up, the quality has not infrequently gone down. Because the vineyard acreage in Burgundy cannot be expanded, there has been a tendency for many growers to produce more wine per acre by not pruning back their vines. If the same vine nourishes more bunches of grapes than it is meant to, the resulting wine will be less intense in character, and its flavor less concentrated and distinct. There are, of course, exact limits of production set by the French government for each *Appellation Contrôlée* wine. In abundant years, however, a certain percentage of the excess production of various appellations is reclassified a few months after the vintage so that it, too, can be sold under the given appellation. Furthermore, if a grower produces more wine than he is legally permitted to from, say, the Perrières vineyard in Meursault, he can still sell the overproduction simply as Meursault, without the vineyard name. And if he produces more Meursault than he should, he can sell the rest as Bourgogne Blanc. This declassification of wine, by which overproduction can spill down into the next lower appellation, permits growers to be sure of selling just about whatever they produce, of both red and white Burgundy. As a result, there is even more reason to choose expensive white Burgundies carefully.

Turning now to the wines mentioned above, Bourgogne Blanc is the basic appellation of white Burgundy. The words Bourgogne Blanc are not often found on a label because, surprisingly enough, there is not a great deal of wine produced with just that appellation. Among red wines, for example, there is ten times as much Bourgogne Rouge made as there is Nuits St.-Georges; among whites, however, there is as much Meursault produced as there is Bourgogne Blanc. On the other hand, the Mâcon district, about halfway between Dijon and Lyon, produces a great deal of pleasant and comparatively inexpensive white wine. The wine has long been shipped here as Mâcon, Mâcon Supérieur, and Mâcon-Villages, the basic difference between the three appellations being that the last two have one degree more alcohol than does Mâcon. In recent years, many shippers have taken to labeling the wine as Pinot Chardonnay, after the grape variety from which it must entirely be made. Even so, the label will contain the *Appellation Contrôlée* of the wine, which will usually be Mâcon and occasionally Bourgogne. Although a Bourgogne Blanc, Mâcon, or Pinot Chardonnay from Burgundy will never be as distinct a wine as a good Meursault or Chablis, it can certainly be a good, clean, well-made example of white Burgundy. Since the wine is made entirely from the best grape variety of all for dry white wines, and since many examples cost $3 to $4, a good Bourgogne Blanc or Mâcon Blanc is not only a good value, but can actually be a better wine than some of the weak or unbalanced examples of more expensive white Burgundy.

Bourgogne Aligoté is a lesser Burgundy, produced from the Aligoté grape, and bears little relation to a true Burgundy made from the Pinot Chardonnay. As it happens, there is a great deal of this wine made—its production far exceeds that of Chablis and Pouilly-Fuissé combined—but it has never been widely marketed here. The wine is rather light, quite pleasant in a good vintage when drunk young, but is not meant to be kept in bottle any period of time. It is therefore a dangerous wine to ship unless it can be consumed fairly quickly. A few stores bring a quantity in from time to time, and the wine occasionally makes its appearance in unusual circumstances. For example, B&G Prince d'Argent is a Bourgogne Aligoté, although it takes a certain amount of squinting to make out the appellation on the label.

Here is a brief selection of less expensive white Burgundies, although at $3.00 to $4.50, these wines are necessarily among the most expensive in this guide.

Bouchard Père	Monopole (Bourgogne Blanc)
Drouhin	Soleil Blanc (Bourgogne Blanc)
Jadot	Mâcon Blanc
Jaffelin	Bourgogne du Chapitre (Bourgogne Blanc)
Latour	Pinot Chardonnay (Bourgogne Blanc)

Muscadet

The Muscadet region, near the mouth of the Loire, takes its name from that of the grape variety used to make its wines. Muscadet is a fresh, light-bodied wine marked by a crisp acidity in most years, and by a softer style if the summer has been especially hot. As this wine has become increasingly popular, first in France, and then in the United States, production has increased to more than five million cases in abundant vintages. Consequently, many examples sell for $3.00 or less, and Muscadet is one of the best values around among dry wines.

The most recent available vintage is the one to look for. Muscadet is usually bottled within months of the vintage, and the vintage date is a reliable guide to the age of the wine, so that you can drink this wine while it is still fresh. This is not always possible with some other dry white wines from Europe, which are aged too long before being bottled, and dated inaccurately.

There are three inner districts within the Muscadet region, of which Sèvre-et-Maine is traditionally considered the best. This distinction is less useful to the consumer than it appears, because for one thing, Sèvre-et-Maine accounts for almost 90 percent of all the Muscadet made.

For another, some of the shippers whose labels do not bear the name of this inner district may nevertheless be using Sèvre-et-Maine wines: they simply feel that using the word Muscadet by itself makes it easier for the consumer to recognize the wine. A Muscadet *sur lie*, on the lees, is one that has been bottled directly from the barrel, without first having been racked—or decanted, so to speak—into another barrel to separate the wine from its natural deposits. A Muscadet *sur lie* theoretically has a more distinct flavor than other Muscadet, as well as a slight *pétillance,* or prickly quality, but it would be very difficult indeed to pick out those wines which have been bottled *sur lie* once they have traveled across the ocean and spent additional months in storage.

Most French shippers now include a Muscadet in their line. Good examples include Domaine de l'Hyvernière, Château du Coin, L'Huitrière, Cuvée des Aigles, and those shipped by Ackerman-Laurance, Barré Frères, and Remy-Pannier.

Sancerre and **Pouilly-Fumé**, from another part of the Loire, are two excellent full-bodied dry white wines with a more distinct flavor than Muscadet. The wines are in limited supply, and the best-known brands now cost $4 or more. If you come across a less expensive example of either wine, it is well worth trying.

Sauternes
Barsac

The Sauternes district, southeast of the city of Bordeaux, produces what are probably the best-known sweet white dessert wines in the world. They are made from ripe grapes that have been left on the vine until they are attacked by *pourriture noble,* or noble rot. This beneficial mold shrivels up the grapes so that they have a higher proportion of sugar and a greater concentration of flavor. Sauternes is made primarily from the Sémillon grape, along with a certain amount of Sauvignon Blanc and Muscadelle. Barsac, one of five communes within the Sauternes district, has become such a famous appellation on its own that although its wines can be sold as Sauternes, they are usually labeled as Barsac.

Sauternes and Barsac are not so popular as they once were, perhaps because people no longer serve a sweet wine with dessert, perhaps because many consumers never drink sweet wines at all. As a result, the best of these wines are to some extent underpriced, even if they exceed our price limits. Regional Sauternes, Barsac, and Haut Sauternes cost $3 to $5. The last is not an official appellation, but if a shipper offers one, it will be sweeter than his Sauternes. Sweet Sauterne from California and New York State costs less, but these wines are also less rich and less complex in taste. Sauternes and Barsac have a distinct and unique taste that comes partly from the soil of the region, partly from the effects of the *pourriture noble,* and this taste cannot be duplicated by wines that are merely sweet. Among regional Sauternes, those shipped by B&G, Cruse, Johnston, de Luze, and Sichel are lighter in style, those of Ginestet and Lichine fuller and somewhat sweeter.

Apart from regional wines, there are a number of château-bottled wines of established reputation that exhibit the characteristics of the region in an even more concentrated way. Château d'Yquem is the most famous, and most expensive, of these wines, but others include Châteaux Coutet, Climens, Guiraud, Rieussec, Suduiraut, and Rayne-Vigneau. Until recently the wines from these classified châteaux were often less expensive than regional

Sauternes from the best-known shippers. This is no longer the case, but if you enjoy these wines enough to shop around, you should be able to find wines from the top châteaux for $4 to $6.

Sweet white wines age better than dry wines, and a five- or ten-year-old Sauternes can be a particularly rich and luscious wine. Remember that the best vintage years for château-bottled Sauternes—regional wines are labeled only with good vintages—are not the same ones as for Graves or red Bordeaux. Finally, since a glass of Sauternes is as much as many people will want with dessert, you may want to buy half-bottles more often than bottles.

Vouvray

Although many people have heard of Vouvray, few seem to drink this appealing, mellow wine from the Loire. Produced entirely from the Chenin Blanc grape, also known locally as the Pineau de la Loire, Vouvray can be dry, semisweet, or sweet. Each of these styles can, in turn, be made into a still wine, one that is *pétillant*, or slightly sparkling, or into a *mousseux*, a fully sparkling wine. The comparative dryness of Vouvray depends partly on the intent of the winemaker, but also on annual variations in climate. In most regions a wine will simply be better or worse depending on the nature of the vintage, but in Vouvray the very style of the wine will vary: light and dry, round and full-bodied, or rich and luscious. Most of the Vouvray shipped here is slightly sweet and still, rather than *pétillant* or sparkling. Vouvray vinified into a dry wine is less appealing, as it tends to lack charm and fruit.

Although Vouvray is an easy name to remember, and the wine itself quite attractive, it has never achieved great popularity here, and there are relatively few brands to choose from. Nevertheless, there are good, relatively mellow examples at $3.25 or so, including those from three Loire shippers, Ackerman-Laurance, Marconnay, and Remy-Pannier.

Anjou Blanc and **Coteaux du Layon** are two other Loire wines made entirely from the Chenin Blanc grape. Although these soft and appealing wines are not often found here, you may come across a bottle that is even less expensive than Vouvray.

ITALY

Frascati

The old, fortified towns in the Alban hills a few miles south of Rome are known as the Castelli Romani, and their vineyards provide the dry and light-bodied white wines served in virtually every Roman restaurant. Although **Castelli Romani** is the general appellation for the wines of all of these towns, the village of Frascati has made a separate—and better-known—name for itself. Frascati is often singled out as exactly the kind of country wine that cannot travel. Surprisingly enough, many examples of Frascati shipped here are among the palest and cleanest of all Italian whites. They have very little flavor—which may be a virtue among the white wines of Italy—but they are not marred by the over-aged character encountered so often. They are not expensive, but you must decide for yourself whether or not it is worth $2 or so to drink wines—however well made—that have so little taste. Bottles that cost much more are perhaps not worth the experiment; less expensive examples have all the faults of cheap wines. The Frascati of Fontana Candida, the Cooperative of Marino, and Valle Vermiglia are well made. The Cooperative also markets a pleasant light wine under the name Marino, which is another of the Castelli Romani villages.

Orvieto

The ancient hill town of Orvieto has given its name to two styles of white wine—*secco*, dry, and *abboccato*, semisweet. It is the *abboccato* that has made the fame of this wine, and its fruit and elegance are such that it may be one of the few semisweet wines that seem to be enjoyed even by those who normally drink dry wines. Nevertheless, more Orvieto *secco* is now being made to conform to the current consumer preference for dry white wines. Orvieto *secco*, like dry Vouvray, is just another white wine, whereas the *abboccato* is a distinct wine with more appeal. Orvieto has traditionally been marketed in *pulcianelli*, squat straw-covered flasks similar to those used for Chianti, but many firms are now using standard bottles and the new, flagon-like *Orvietela*.

Since most brands now sell for $3 or more, even Orvieto *abboccato* is not the best value among semisweet wines, but it is different enough to be worth trying. Bigi is less expensive than the others, which include Antinori, Melini, Petrurbani, and Ruffino.

Other semisweet Italian wines include Antinori Bianco della Costa Toscana (in a distinctive fish-shaped bottle), Melini Lacrima d'Arno, Riunite Scandiano Bianco Amabile, and Bon-Sol Alpino Bianco, which is the least expensive of the four.

Soave

Soave, the best-selling white wine of Italy, deserves its popularity. It is generally the most successful of Italian whites, and the best-known shippers are also the most dependable. How good a value Soave is compared to other dry white wines is another matter.

At its best, Soave is pale in color, light-bodied, and pleasantly dry; it is not a wine with a marked personality or depth of flavor. As it ages, Soave may gain a bit in fullness of flavor, but it gradually loses the charm and freshness that are its chief virtues. Fortunately, the Italian tradition of over-aging white wines and of blending in a certain proportion of older wines to add body is no longer prevalent among the major producers. For that reason, and also because they have a faster turnover, wines from such firms as Bertani, Bolla, Ruffino, and Antinori are likely to be fresher and better made. At $2.75 to $3.25, however, Soave is not a bargain, and you may find less expensive fresh, dry wines from other countries that are equally enjoyable. In any case, cheaper examples of Soave are not a solution—such wines are more often than not weak in flavor, if not poorly made.

Verdicchio is easily recognized by the distinctive amphora-like bottle in which it is sold. It is a wine with somewhat more body than Soave, and costs about the same. Fazi-Battaglia is the most popular brand, Aurora and Umani Ronchi are less expensive.

The most widely distributed group of Italian white wines, apart from Soave and Verdicchio, are those marketed by the firms that make Chianti. At one time there was a certain amount of White Chianti shipped here. The new wine laws have now made it illegal to use this appellation, so the Chianti producers now label their white wines either as Tuscan White Wine or simply as Bianco. Ruffino Bianco and Toscano White Wine, Frescobaldi Pomino, and Brolio Bianco are among the dry wines available in bottles and in *fiaschi*. They are well-made and pleasant enough, a change from Soave, but no less expensive.

GERMANY

RHINE:	MOSELLE:
Liebfraumilch	**Bernkasteler**
Niersteiner	**Piesporter**
Johannisberger	**Zeltinger**
Rüdesheimer	**Graacher**
	Zeller Schwarze Katz
	Kröver Nacktarsch

Whether or not one agrees with the enthusiasts who rate the white wines of Germany as the finest in the world, it is fair to say that they have a distinctive style and charm that is virtually unique. Rhines and Moselles are all characterized by a fragrant and flowery style combined with a more-or-less harmonious balance of sweetness and acidity. Cheap German wines can be rather pale in color and light in body, without much flavor of any kind. Others may be sweet and dull, or thin and acid. This suggests that although German wines can be found for as little as $1.49, a more realistic minimum for a well-made Rhine or Moselle might be $2.75 or $3. It would be a mistake to assume that because German wines have an over-all similarity, an inexpensive bottle tastes about the same as one that costs $1 or $2 more.

Unfortunately, selecting the best German wines is not simply a matter of spending more money. Understanding German wine labels requires more knowledge than most people care to acquire, even if they realize that the style of these wines cannot be matched in any other wine region. There are a greater number of important wine villages in Germany than in Burgundy, and more individual vineyards of note than in Bordeaux. Furthermore, most German vineyards are split up among several owners, each of whom will make a somewhat different wine. To complicate matters even more, German winemakers traditionally produce not one but several different wines from the same vineyard in every good vintage, by making successive pickings of increasingly ripe grapes.

As a result of this discouraging complexity, German wine shippers and most consumers have limited their attention to just a few regional appellations, the most popular of which are listed at the head of this section. Since these appellations account for more than 80 percent of the German wines sold here, and since they are by far the most widely available German wines, they are described here as a single category.

With the exception of Liebfraumilch, which comes from vineyards situated in the principal districts along the Rhine, regional wines are marketed with the name of a specific village: Bernkasteler, Johannisberger, Niersteiner, and so on. This concentration on just a handful of names, which ignores dozens of wine villages and hundreds of vineyards, certainly simplifies the marketing of German wines. Given the nature of regional wines, selecting from among even these few names can be further simplified. As it happens, a wine labeled with the name of a specific village does not have to be made entirely with wines from that village, so that there is less of a difference than one might suppose between wines bearing the names of neighboring villages, such as Bernkasteler and Piesporter, or Johannisberger and Rüdesheimer. The biggest difference among the regional wines of any particular shipper is that between the light-bodied, slightly tart, fresh wines of the Moselle (in green bottles) and the softer, fuller, somewhat sweeter wines of the Rhine (in brown bottles).

Another distinction that cuts across individual village appellations is that between wines made primarily from the Riesling grape and those made primarily from the Sylvaner. The Riesling, which generally produces wines with more finesse and elegance, is the most widely cultivated grape variety along the Moselle, and in such Rhine villages as Johannisberg and Rüdesheim. These wines are therefore likely to have more distinction than those made primarily from the Sylvaner, such as Liebfraumilch and Niersteiner. If the word Riesling actually appears on a regional label—as in Bernkasteler Riesling or Johannisberger Riesling—at least 75 percent of that wine must be made from that grape variety.

Regional wines may also be labeled with a combination of a village name and that of a vineyard, and this can lead to some confusion. As is the case in Bordeaux and Burgundy, the finest German wines come from a limited number of specific vineyards whose labels carry not only the vineyard name but also that of the village in which it is situated. Ockfener Bockstein, Rauenthaler Baiken, Forster Jesuitengarten, Graacher Himmelreich, and Johannisberger Klaus are some examples of single vineyard wines from the villages of Ockfen, Rauenthal, Forst, and so on. There are some exceptions to this method of labeling—the names of such famous vineyards as Schloss Vollrads, Schloss Johannisberg, Steinberg, and Scharzhofberg are not preceded by the name of the village in which each is located—but the combination of village plus vineyard is almost always used for single vineyard wines. Consequently, wines labeled Bernkasteler Badstube Niersteiner Auflangen, Johannisberger Erntebringer, Hochheimer Daubhaus, Piesporter Michelsberg, and Rauenthaler Steinmächer, to take just a few examples, would appear to come from individual vineyards. In fact, these are regional appellations which have been permitted almost as much flexibility of origin as if the wines were simply labeled Bernkasteler, Niersteiner, Johannisberger, and so on.

The fact that regional appellations are less accurate than they appear, even though there are so few of them, suggests that differences in quality depend more on the shipper or the brand than on the exact appellation being used. While there is an upper limit to the quality and distinction of a regional wine—so that $4 or more seems a lot to pay—there is not necessarily a bottom limit either to quality or price. It is safer to pay $2.75 to $3.75 for regional Rhines and Moselles from reputable shippers than to buy very cheap examples. Although even well-made regional wines generally lack the concentration of flavor, distinct personality, and finesse that characterize good single-vineyard wines, the wines listed below are nevertheless typical of the style, dependable, and widely available.

The following selection includes well-made Rhines and Moselles that are generally available at $3 to $4.

Deinhard	Hanns Christof Liebfraumilch
	Bernkasteler Green Label
Kayser	Bernkasteler Urglueck
	Liebfraumilch Glockenspiel

Kendermann	Bernkasteler Riesling
	Liebfraumilch Black Tower
Langenbach	Bernkasteler Riesling Meister Krone
Langguth	Piesporter Riesling
	Bernkasteler Riesling Landvogt
Madrigal	Johannisberger Riesling
	Bernkasteler Riesling
Sichel	Blue Nun Liebfraumilch
	Bernkasteler Riesling
Valckenberg	Bernkasteler Falkenkrone

NOTE: The new German wine laws, effective with the 1971 vintage, have redefined the geographical limits of regional appellations, but it is too soon to tell how this will affect the marketing and quality of these wines. The 1971 vintage is of such exceptional quality that it does not represent the typical style of the various appellations or of the new quality levels described in the next section. It is likely that the 1972 wines, which will not be widely available until 1974, will provide the first real look at the effects of the new laws on regional appellations. Nevertheless, the basic changes are worth noting here. Within some regions, the name of its most famous village may now be used for wines from several adjoining villages. Thus the appellation Bereich Johannisberg (*bereich* means district) encompasses wines produced in about fifteen villages in the Rheingau; Bereich Nierstein includes a dozen villages in the Rheinhessen; and Bereich Bernkastel about twenty villages along the Moselle. Similarly, a number of adjoining vineyards may now be labeled with the name of the best-known one among them. For example, within Bereich Johannisberg, the appellation Johannisberger Erntebringer includes wines from six adjoining vineyards, and within Bereich Bernkastel, the appellation Piesporter Michelsberg encompasses seven vineyards. In effect, an appellation such as Bernkastel or Johannisberg has been geographically expanded, whereas the regional appellations made up of village and vineyard names have been more strictly defined. It is likely that the number of different regional appellations marketed by the leading German wine shippers will be reduced, and that the choice of appellations will differ somewhat from those in use now.

Single Vineyard Wines

Single vineyard wines from the top wine estates of Germany are generally harder to find than those of the best vineyards of Bordeaux and Burgundy. On the other hand, stores that do carry a wide selection of estate-bottled German wines will usually have several examples on hand that are actually less expensive than many brands of Liebfraumilch and Bernkasteler. Anyone who wants to drink the best of these wines must learn the names of the top estates and vineyards, but the new German wine laws that went into effect with the 1971 vintage have narrowed the search to some extent.

German wines are now divided into three specific levels of quality, and the appropriate designation appears on each label. *Deutscher Tafelwein,* or German table wine, includes the least interesting wines, and very little is shipped here. *Qualitätswein bestimmter Anbaugebiete,* or quality wine from delimited districts, accounts for almost all German shipments, since most regional wines are included in this category. There are eleven delimited districts set up within the *Qualitätswein,* or *QbA,* category, the best known of which are Moselle-Saar-Ruwer, Rheingau, Rheinhessen, Rheinpfalz, and Nahe. The district of origin appears on each label, so that a consumer can determine where a wine comes from, even if it bears an unfamiliar village or vineyard name.

The finest wines are labeled *Qualitätswein mit Prädikat*, or quality wine with special attributes. The special attributes are those which have always been associated with the very best wines: Kabinett, Spätlese, Auslese, Beerenauslese, and Trockenbeerenauslese. These designations take into account the fact that the quality of the finest German wines depends not simply on the excellence of the vineyard site but also on the relative ripeness of the grapes when they are picked. Spätlese, or late-picked, indicates that the wine has been made from especially ripe grapes that were picked after the normal harvest. Auslese, or selected picking, designates a wine made from specially selected bunches of extra-ripe grapes. Beerenauslese and Trockenbeerenauslese wines are very sweet, and very expensive, wines made from overripe, shriveled grapes picked one by one.

Qualitätswein mit Prädikat on a label is a clear indication that the wine is in the top rank, that it has been made from fully ripe grapes, and that it is therefore likely to have the concentration of flavor and the finesse that characterizes the best of German wines. Within this category, Kabinett wines are the least sweet, and a Spätlese or Auslese from the Moselle-Saar-Ruwer will generally be less sweet than a Rhine wine so labeled. As to estate bottling, a wine whose label bears the words *Aus dem eigene Lesegut,* from his own property, or *Erzeuger-abfüllung,* his own bottling, followed by the name of the producer, indicates authentic estate bottling, as *Originalabfüllung* did in the past. *Aus dem Lesegut von,* from the vineyard of, indicates only who made the wine, but not who bottled it. Such a label also bears the word *abfüllung,* bottled, followed by the name of a shipper.

SPAIN

Rioja

The dry white wines of Rioja are generally less successful than the reds. Some are aged too long and lack freshness and delicacy; others are soundly made but dull in taste, without much charm or lively acidity. Some exceptions are noted below.

On the other hand, the semisweet wines of this region can be very attractive. If you enjoy wines similar in style to a light Sauterne or a California Sweet Semillon, you will find some good values from the Rioja *bodegas.* Unfortunately the label does not usually indicate which wines are dry and which are not, but in the following list the semisweet wines are indicated with an *. Most of these wines cost less than $2.50, some less than $2.

Bodegas Bilbainas

    Viña Paceta
    Cepa de Oro
    Brillante*

Bodegas Franco-Españolas
Bodegas Gomez Cruzado
Bodegas Riojanas
Bodegas Unidas
Compañía Vinicola del
    Norte de España (Cune)

    Diamante*
    Spanish Chablis
    Monte Real*
    AGE

    Rioja Blanco
    Monopole

Federico Paternina	Banda Dorada
	Monte Haro*
Lopez de Heredia	Viña Tondonia
Marqués de Murrieta	Rioja Blanco

PORTUGAL

Vinho Verde

The Vinho Verde district in northern Portugal produces both red and white wines, but only the white is shipped to this country. Vinho Verde means green wine, but only in the sense of young wine, and many examples found in Portugal have a crisp, slightly tart quality, combined with a refreshing sprightliness that explains the unusual name of this wine. The Vinho Verde that is sold here often exhibits a very mild sparkle—more apparent on the tongue than in the glass—but the wine itself is often neutral and mildly sweet. As such, it will appeal to many as a pleasant, if undistinguished, white wine: at $2.25 to $3 a bottle, it is unusual enough to seek out. Casal Garcia, from the Aveleda estate, is the best known Vinho Verde, and there are many other dependable examples, including Lagosta and Moura Basto.

The white wines of Dão are starting to appear, but they are generally less appealing than those of Vinho Verde; the latter region makes better white wines, as Dão makes better reds.

YUGOSLAVIA

Šipon from Maribor
Šipon from Ormoz
Laski-Rizling from Jeruzalem
Rizling from Fruška-Gora
Traminec from Radgona
Rizvanac from Slavonia
Sauvignon from Fruška-Gora

There is a wider range of Yugoslavian white wines available than of reds, and if they are not all consistently interesting, the group nevertheless includes several distinct white wines at $2. The selection above consists of the most interesting of these wines. The unfamiliar varietal names used in Yugoslavia—those listed above and others you may come across—require some clarification. Rizling, Laški-Rizling, and Graševina are the same grape, but none is the Riesling of Germany; it is the Italian Riesling which is widely planted in Yugoslavia, and which produces a pleasant enough wine that naturally lacks the fruit and breed of the true Riesling. Rizvanac is the Muller-Thurgau, a cross between the Riesling and Sylvaner; Traminec (pronounced traminets) is the Traminer of Alsace and retains the distinctive bouquet and style of that wine. Šipon (pronounced shee-pon) is vinified to produce two different wines: the Šipon of Maribor is a mild, slightly sweet wine, the Šipon of Ormoz is much fuller and sweeter.

All the wines listed are available under the Adriatica label, which is the principal brand under which Yugoslavian wines are now sold here. The varietal wines offered under the Navip and Slovin labels tend to duplicate those in the Adriatica line, even if the place of origin seems to differ. You are therefore as likely to enjoy one as well as another, and your choice of brand name really depends on what you find available on the shelf.

HUNGARY

Debröi Hárslevelü
Badacsonyi Szürkebarát
Csopaki Olaszrizling

The most famous wine of Hungary is Tokay, a sweet dessert wine described below. The white table wines of Hungary are by no means dry and crisp, however, and are described by their advocates as ripe and luscious. If you care to try this kind of wine, Debröi Hárslevelü (the wine comes from Debro, and is made from the Hárslevelü grape) is the fullest and roundest wine of the group. Badacsonyi Szürkebarát is a soft, slightly mellow wine, and the third selection is a light, mild wine with a muted flowery style. All three cost $3 or so.

Tokay at its finest is priced well beyond our limits, but as there are six different labelings of Tokay shipped to this country, a few words of advice may be of use. The reputation of this sweet wine has been made from Tokay Aszu—other Tokays are more or less dry and much less interesting. Tokaji Aszu, as it is spelled on the label, is available here in three grades—three, four, and five *put-tonys*—the last being the sweetest, richest, and most honeyed. It costs about $6 for a 16-ounce bottle, but less expensive Tokay may leave you wondering why the wine is so famous.

AUSTRIA

Gumpoldskirchner

About 90 percent of Austrian wines are white, and although they are not widely available here, they are pleasant and enjoyable wines that sell for $2 to $3. It is the custom in Vienna for local taverns to offer the new wines, or *heurige*, within weeks of the vintage. These are light, fresh, sprightly wines that are meant to be consumed casually and copiously. The Austrian wines shipped here seem to be fuller-bodied, and are often labeled Spätlese or Auslese, which indicates that the wines are comparatively mellow in style. They are agreeable nevertheless, and will appeal to anyone who prefers wines that are not entirely dry.

Just south of Vienna is the village of Gumpoldskirchen, whose wines are perhaps the best known of all, and most easily found in this country. Spätlese and Spätlese Cabinet are to be seen on many labels, and the wines are generally mild, slightly mellow, and most agreeable when young. Some producers whose wines are priced at $3 or less are Weigl, Juch, and Schwanberg. **Nussberger** and **Grinzinger**, from two towns on the northern edge of Vienna, are lighter in body than Gumpoldskirchner, and some examples are crisply dry.

GREECE

White Wines

The best known white wine of Greece is **retsina**, an unusual and pungent wine made by adding pine resin to the fermenting must. Anyone who drinks retsina regularly is likely to find all of the other wines of the world—how shall I put it?—unnecessarily subtle. Many people drink retsina occasionally with Greek food, however, and if you enjoy this wine it does have the advantage of low price. Most retsina is sold in quart bottles for $2.50 or so, which is the equivalent of $1.85 a bottle. Almost all the retsina sold here is white, although there is also some light red retsina labeled Kokkineli.

Greek white wines other than retsina are less of a value than the reds. Although they are full-flavored, they tend to be aged too long before being bottled, and they all seem to retain a slightly resinated taste. The best-known white wines include Demestica and Sta. Helena of Achaia, Clauss; Hymettus of Cambas; and Robola and Mont Ambelos of Nicolaou.

UNITED STATES

CALIFORNIA:

Chablis
Sauterne and Dry Sauterne
Rhine Wine
Mountain White

Many examples of California Chablis are no more than neutral, acceptable dry wines without any distinguishing style of their own. There are, however, a number of wineries that produce fresh, crisp white wines with enough acidity to set them off as very good values. These wines can be favorably compared with any number of well-known dry white wines which cost more but which are not as well made. Although there are a number of red wines which are more attractive and less expensive than California Burgundy, most of the world's white wines have little to recommend them except a fresh and lively taste. In this context, the technological skills of California winemakers enable them to compete both in quality and in price.

California Chablis are listed in three price groups; the wines in the third group are the least expensive and least dry.

Beaulieu Vineyard Chablis
Charles Krug Chablis
Christian Brothers Chablis
Inglenook Vintage Chablis
Paul Masson Chablis
Mirassou Chablis
Wente Bros. Chablis

Almadén Mountain White Chablis
Beringer Mountain White Chablis
Martini Mountain White Wine (Chablis)

Franzia Chablis
Gallo Chablis Blanc
Italian Swiss Colony Napa-Sonoma-Mendocino Chablis

There are only a few California Rhine wines. The most interesting are the light, fragrant Inglenook Navalle Rhine and the sweet, honeyed Paul Masson Rhine Castle, which contains an agreeable trace of Muscat. Oddly enough, Christian Brothers Sauterne and Italian Swiss Colony Haut Sauterne both have the mildly sweet taste and distinctly fragrant bouquet of Rhine wines, despite their labels. The Italian Swiss Colony wine, which is available in gallons, is appealing and inexpensive—an excellent value if you enjoy this style of wine.

California Rhine wines are listed in descending order of price.

> Christian Brothers Sauterne
> Paul Masson Rhine Castle and Rhine
> Inglenook Navalle Rhine
> Italian Swiss Colony Haut Sauterne

Sauterne and Dry Sauterne (sometimes spelled with the final *s*) are puzzling appellations in California, because these wines are almost invariably as dry as those marketed as Chablis. The Dry Sauterne of Masson and of Charles Krug, for example, are well-made dry wines—but isn't it less confusing to buy their equally well-made Chablis? Semillon and Dry Semillon are varietal wines similar in style to a Dry Sauterne, and some labels display both the generic and varietal appellations together: Almadén Dry Semillon Sauterne, Beaulieu Vineyard Dry Sauterne Semillon. However they are labeled, these are usually undistinguished dry wines. Two exceptions are the distinctive Dry Semillon of Inglenook and Wente Bros.

CALIFORNIA:

Sweet Sauterne and Haut Sauterne
Sweet Semillon
Sweet Sauvignon Blanc
Chateau Wines

The usual distinction between generic and varietal wines is blurred in the case of the sweet white wines of

126

California. Some wineries also use a Chateau name, such as Chateau Concannon, Chateau Beaulieu, and Chateau Masson, to indicate their sweetest wine in the Sauterne category. Since these three approaches to labeling are sometimes combined on a single label, it is sometimes difficult to tell just how sweet any wine is, and which are the sweetest wines of all. Wente sells a Dry Semillon, a Semillon-Haut Sauterne, and a Chateau Semillon, which is the sweetest of all, although not nearly as sweet as Chateau Concannon-Haut Sauterne. Paul Masson Chateau Masson is not especially sweet, and Beaulieu Vineyard Chateau Beaulieu-Sauvignon Blanc is sweeter than their Haut Sauternes-Sweet Sauternes. In addition, some wineries market a dry Sauvignon Blanc, others produce a sweet wine with the same varietal name.

By way of putting these wines into some perspective, the best of them are well-made, well-balanced semisweet wines. Except for Chateau Concannon, these wines are not as sweet as a Sauternes or Barsac from France, and may therefore be overwhelmed by a very sweet dessert. A popular and appealing sweet wine, with a taste different from those listed below, is Christian Brothers Chateau La Salle, made primarily from Muscat grapes.

Beaulieu Vineyard	Chateau Beaulieu-Sauvignon Blanc
Christian Brothers	Sauvignon Blanc
Concannon	Chateau Concannon-Haut Sauterne
Charles Krug	Sweet Sauternes Sauvignon Blanc
Wente Bros.	Chateau Semillon

127

CALIFORNIA:

Pinot Chardonnay
Chenin Blanc
Sauvignon Blanc
Johannisberg Riesling
Riesling, Sylvaner, and Riesling-Sylvaner
Gewürztraminer and Traminer

There are more white varietal wines than reds produced in California, and they, too, originated in different European wine districts. Pinot Chardonnay and Pinot Blanc come from Burgundy; Sauvignon Blanc and Sémillon from Bordeaux; the Riesling (marketed in California as Johannisberg Riesling or White Riesling) and the Sylvaner (usually sold as Riesling) both come from Germany; Traminer and Gewürztraminer come from Alsace. Two other varietal wines, each associated with an individual winery, are Pineau de la Loire of The Christian Brothers, and Folle Blanche of Louis Martini.

Although many different white varietal wines are available from the leading California wineries, many of them are comparatively neutral in style. Part of the reason is that certain varieties do not have a clearly defined taste, and part is the intent of some wineries to make clean white wines without much varietal character. Consequently you may find several well-made California Chablis, listed on page 125, to be as attractive as many varietally labeled wines—and less expensive.

The Pinot Chardonnay is the most successful varietal white wine of California, but most examples are expensive, as are many excellent Johannisberg Rieslings. Good values are to be found in Chenin Blanc, Gewürztraminer and Traminer, Pinot Blanc, and dry Sauvignon Blanc (sometimes marketed as Blanc Fumé). Dry Semillon is less successful than Sweet Semillon, described elsewhere. The Sylvaner, usually marketed as Riesling or as Riesling-Sylvaner, is an agreeable wine, although perhaps less of a value than Alsatian Sylvaner. Green Hungarian is a neutral and uninteresting wine, not nearly as attractive as its name. Grey Riesling, not a Riesling at all, is a fairly dull white wine, although one or two examples do have a fresh, dry taste. Pineau de la Loire and White Pinot are actually the Chenin Blanc. Emerald Riesling is a cross between the Riesling of Germany and the Muscadelle: the best-known example is sold by Paul Masson as Emerald Dry.

The following selection of varietal white wines does not necessarily include the very best examples produced in California, but simply some of the best wines generally available for $2.25 to $3.75.

Almadén	Blanc Fumé
	Gewürztraminer
Beaulieu Vineyard	Johannisberg Riesling
	Sylvaner-Riesling
Beringer	Chenin Blanc
Christian Brothers	Chenin Blanc
	Johannisberg Riesling
	Pinot Chardonnay
Inglenook	Chenin Blanc
Charles Krug	Chenin Blanc
	Gewürztraminer
	Sylvaner-Riesling
Martini	Dry Chenin Blanc
	Gewürztraminer
	Johannisberg Riesling

Paul Masson	Pinot Blanc
	Chenin Blanc
	Riesling
	Emerald Dry
Mirassou	Chenin Blanc
	Monterey Riesling
	Gewürztraminer
Robert Mondavi	Riesling
	Chenin Blanc
	Fumé Blanc
Sebastiani	Chenin Blanc
	Gewürztraminer
Wente Bros.	Blanc de Blancs
	Sauvignon Blanc

NEW YORK STATE:

Chablis
Sauterne
White Wine

The pronounced flavor and comparatively sweet taste of New York State wines has already been described on page 95. Attractive examples of white wines from the four major producers include Taylor Lake Country White, Great Western Pleasant Valley White Niagara and Aurora Sauterne, Widmer Lake Niagara and Dry Sauterne, and Gold Seal Catawba White.

Dry white wines include the delicate and appealing Charles Fournier Chablis Nature of Gold Seal, and the fuller-flavored White Wine of Boordy Vineyards and Bully Hill.

Rosés

Rosés of the World

Rosé has become a popular wine only in the past thirty years or so, and it has come in for more than its share of snubs. Many wine drinkers never drink rosé at all, others drink very little else, at least partly on the assumption that it goes well with everything. One French writer has suggested, however, that it would be more accurate to say that rosé goes with nothing, except perhaps certain foods with which wine is inappropriate—salads, hors d'oeuvres, cold cuts, spicy foods, and so on. To be fair, rosés complement not only certain dishes, but also many casual occasions that call for no more than a refreshing beverage. An adventuresome wine drinker might complain that when there are so many interesting red and white wines to choose from, rosés need not serve so often as an uncertain compromise. Nevertheless, rosés are such popular and appealing wines, and their success depends so much on brand promotion, distinctive names, unusual bottles, and a certain amount of snobbery, that they are well worth examining—as is rarely done—from the point of view of quality and price.

A sommelier once remarked that a rosé is everything but a wine. More accurately, rosé is an incomplete red wine, since the grape skins that gradually impart color to red wines during fermentation are removed after a day or so, when the wine has achieved an appropriate pink color. Since the best grape varieties are rarely used, and since the early removal of the grape skins results in wines with little body and character, rosés generally have less individuality of taste than most red and white wines.

Of course, there are other ways of making rosé, as I discovered to my embarrassment when I was shown around the bottling facilities of a Portuguese rosé shipper. My guide explained that the organization of the bottling line could be followed easily by a master chart on the wall that indicated the location of every lot of incoming wine—red lines for the reds, yellow lines for the whites.

"But where are the pink lines for the rosés?" I asked. The guide stared at me in disbelief, and as I realized that this rosé was made by mixing red and white wines together, my face turned the color of the bottled wine.

If you accept the view that however appealing rosés are, few of them are distinguished, then the simplest way to approach these wines as a group is to divide them into those that are dry, and those that are more or less sweet. Within the second category, rosés are to a large extent interchangeable. Sweet wines are much less distinct in taste than dry wines, and most sweet rosés are as neutral as they are mellow. Consequently there is no need to spend more than, say, $2.50 for a mellow rosé, if that much. Dry rosés are only somewhat less interchangeable, and in any case many consumers would find it difficult to justify paying much more than $3 for a bottle of rosé based on the taste of the wine alone. Since good values can be found among the most easily available rosés, there is no reason to search out such unusual or expensive wines as Vin Gris from Alsace, Oeil de Perdrix from Switzerland, Roditis from Greece, Rosado from Rioja, Opolo from Yugoslavia, Chiaretto from Lake Garda, and so on.

Among widely available dry rosés, those from California offer the best values, and some are listed at the end of this section. Côtes de Provence and Tavel are the best-known dry rosés from France. Provence rosés, usually shipped in distinctive bottles, are pleasant enough, but those from the best-known estates cost $3 to $4. Tavel is the most highly acclaimed of all dry rosés, but most examples now cost $3.50 to $4.50. Furthermore, a full-flavored expensive rosé is something of a contradiction. If it is meant to accompany picnic food, why not get a different dry rosé for half the price? If it is chosen for its comparatively full flavor, why not buy a less expensive light red wine and cool it down? If you insist on Tavel, Château d'Aquéria is an excellent example, as are those shipped by Delas and Chapoutier.

There is a greater choice available among semisweet rosés, including those from Portugal, the Anjou region of France, New York State, and California. Portuguese rosés are mild, mellow wines, and some are very lightly sparkling. Mateus, the most popular, is as good as any, and better than many. Less expensive Portuguese rosés include the slightly sweeter Doña Maria and Grandélite; Lagosta and Pombal, which have a little more flavor; and Costa do Sol, shipped in a quart bottle, and good value.

Anjou Rosé, the most widely available French rosé, is

about as sweet as those from Portugal. Among the widely distributed brands are Nectarose, Château de Tigné, Blanchard Half-Dry, and those shipped by Lichine and de Luze. The neutral style of Anjou Rosé is such, however, that less expensive brands are often as appealing as those that cost more—which is certainly not the case with a dry rosé such as Tavel.

The sweetest rosés of all come from New York State. Widmer's Lake Roselle, Taylor Lake Country Pink, Great Western Isabella Rosé, and Gold Seal Catawba Pink are all well made, but much sweeter than those from Portugal or Anjou.

The rosés of California, many of them available in gallon and half-gallon jugs, include a certain variety of price and taste. The least expensive, such as Pink Chablis from Gallo and Italian Swiss Colony, are appealing sweet rosés marked by a fruity, berrylike quality. At the other end of the spectrum are such distinctive varietal rosés as the dry Petite Rosé of Mirassou, and the less dry Gamay Rosé of Robert Mondavi. In between are an assortment of mellow and dry rosés, some of which are listed below. Some semisweet rosés from California seem to have more flavor than those from Portugal or Anjou; none are as sweet as the best-selling examples from New York State.

Dry Rosés

Almadén	Grenache Rosé
Beaulieu Vineyard	Beaurosé
	Grenache Rosé
Christian Brothers	Vin Rosé
Inglenook	Navalle Rosé
Charles Krug	Vin Rosé
Martini	Mountain Vin Rosé

Paul Masson	Vin Rosé Sec
Mirassou	Petite Rosé
Wente Bros.	Rosé Wente
Semisweet Rosés	
Christian Brothers	Napa Rosé
Robert Mondavi	Gamay Rosé
Franzia	Vin Rosé
Gallo	Pink Chablis
Italian Swiss Colony	Pink Chablis

Appendixes

120 Inexpensive Red, White, and Rosé Wines

The selection below is representative of the wines described in this book that cost less than $3.50. It is meant to suggest the variety of sources from which inexpensive wines are available, and the appropriate page numbers for red and white wines are therefore indicated to provide additional examples and commentary. All rosés are described in the section that begins on page 131.

Rather than arrange all of these wines by color alone, I have attempted to group them by taste. These groupings must necessarily be somewhat arbitrary and subjective, especially since some red wines—such as Beaujolais, Barbera, California Zinfandel, and Rioja—can be either light-bodied or full-bodied, and some white wines—such as Graves, Vouvray, and Rioja—can be more or less dry, depending on the intent of the winemaker. Nevertheless, I felt that these groupings, each of which is arranged in ascending order of price, would provide a useful starting point for further explorations.

APPENDIXES

Light-bodied Red Wines

Winemaster's Guild Burgundy, 89
AGE Rioja, 81
CK Mondavi Burgundy, 89
Bon-Sol Rojo Montaña, 82
René Barbier Tinto, 81
Castillo de Mudela Valdepeñas, 81
Christian Brothers Claret, 90
Bersano Barbera Tranquillo, 72
Martini Mountain Claret, 90
Dulong Beaujolais, 56
Borgogno Barbera, 72
Beaulieu Vineyard Gamay Beaujolais, 94
Robert Mondavi Gamay, 95
Bertani Valpolicella, 76
Prosper Maufoux Beaujolais-Brouilly, 56
Loron Morgon, 56

Dry Red Wines

Undurraga Cabernet Reservado, 86
Boordy Vineyards Red Wine, 96
Cambas Pendeli, 85
Adriatica Cabernet from Istria, 83
Concha y Toro Cabernet Sauvignon, 86
Navip Gamay from Venčac, 83
Pagni Chianti, 75
Cune Rioja Clarete, 81
Bigi Chianti, 75
Martini Zinfandel, 95
Achaia, Clauss Castel Danielis, 85
de Luze Club Claret, 62
Beringer Zinfandel, 94
Château Cantegrive, 64
Egri Bikavér, 84
Lichine Médoc, 62
Château Timberlay, 64
Christian Brothers Cabernet Sauvignon, 94
B & G Prince Noir, 61

Ackerman-Laurance Chinon, 69
Château Guiraud-Cheval-Blanc, 64

Full-bodied Red Wines

Gallo Hearty Burgundy, 89
Great Western Chelois, 96
Real Vinicola Dão Cabido, 82
La Vieille Ferme Côtes-du-Rhône, 71
Charles Krug Burgundy, 90
Bodegas Bilbainas Viña Pomal, 80
Delas Côtes-du-Rhône, 71
Beaulieu Vineyard Burgundy, 90
Paternina Banda Azul, 81
Sichel Corbières, 70
Grão Vasco Dão, 82
Nino Negri Inferno, 76
Marqués de Riscal Rioja, 81

Semisweet Red Wines

Taylor Lake Country Red, 96
Great Western Pleasant Valley Red, 96
Riunite Lambrusco, 75
Calissano Lambrusco, 75

Light-bodied Dry White Wines

Martini Mountain White, 125
Gold Seal Chablis Nature, 130
Cune Rioja Blanco, 119
Paul Masson Chablis, 125
Adriatica Rizling from Fruska-Gora, 121
Valle Vermiglia Frascati, 110
Beaulieu Vineyard Chablis, 125
Wente Blanc de Blancs, 130
Cantina Sociale di Marino Frascati, 110
Ackerman-Laurance Muscadet, 106
Willm Cordon d'Alsace, 98
Hugel Sylvaner, 98

APPENDIXES

Ruffino Bianco, 112
Aurora Verdicchio, 111
Trimbach Sylvaner, 98
Barré Frères Muscadet, 106
Bolla Soave, 111

Full-bodied Dry White Wines

Nicolaou Robola, 124
Bodegas Bilbaina Viña Paceta, 119
Almadén Blanc Fumé
Achaia, Clauss Sta. Helena, 124
Inglenook Dry Semillon, 126
Brolio Bianco, 112
Drouhin Soleil Blanc, 105
Ginestet Sauvignon Blanc, 101
Martini Gewürztraminer, 129
Robert Mondavi Fumé Blanc, 130

Semisweet White Wines

Italian Swiss Colony Haut Sauterne, 126
Inglenook Navalle Rhine, 126
Adriatica Sipon from Maribor, 121
Sebastiani Chenin Blanc, 130
Bigi Orvieto *abboccato*, 110
Paul Masson Emerald Dry, 130
Nathaniel Johnston Graves, 102
Langguth Piesporter Riesling, 116
Lagosta Vinho Verde, 120
Bodegas Bilbainas Brillante, 119
Château Malleprat, 102
Remy-Pannier Vouvray, 109
Schwanberg Gumpoldskirchner, 123
Kendermann Bernkasteler Riesling, 116
Debröi Hárslevelü, 122
Christian Brothers Johannisberg Riesling, 129
Mirassou Monterey Riesling, 130
Deinhard Bernkasteler Green Label, 115

Sweet White Wines

Great Western Aurora Sauterne, 130
Widmer Lake Niagara, 130
Paul Masson Rhine Castle, 126
Christian Brothers Chateau La Salle, 127
Wente Chateau Semillon, 127
Paternina Monte Haro Rioja, 120
Charles Krug Sauvignon Blanc, 127
Lichine Sauternes, 107
Beaulieu Vineyard Chateau Beaulieu, 127

Semisweet Rosés

Gallo Pink Chablis
Taylor Lake Country Pink
Widmer Lake Roselle
Christian Brothers Napa Rosé
de Luze Rosé d'Anjou
Costa do Sol Portuguese Rosé
Lichine Rosé d'Anjou
Mateus Portuguese Rosé

Dry Rosés

Inglenook Navalle Rosé
Paul Masson Vin Rosé Sec
Beaulieu Vineyard Grenache Rosé
Charles Krug Vin Rosé

50 Wines in Gallons and Half-gallons

I recall what the proprietor of a Bordeaux vineyard once told me when he fired his cellar master for drunkenness. It was not simply that the man had become inefficient, explained the proprietor, but that he could no longer tell good wine from bad. The cellar master siphoned off a little wine from one or another barrel every day, and since he drank the wine continually, he was unable to perceive the point at which the wine in a particular partially emptied barrel had turned sour.

The drunken cellar master's problem is one that occurs more frequently than you might suppose among people who buy gallon jugs of wine. They begin by drinking glasses of inexpensive wine, and end up drinking glasses of expensive vinegar. Many of them are under the mistaken impression that cheap wine in big bottles does not turn sour. It does. If wine is exposed to air, as in a half-empty jug, it will oxidize as surely—although not as quickly—as a freshly cut apple. There is not always room in the refrigerator for gallon jugs, and even if there were, the air in a partially emptied bottle would still affect the wine adversely. The simplest solution, and the only one that makes sense if you do not plan to drink a gallon at a time, is to decant the wine into smaller bottles as soon as you open the jug. If you don't have wine bottles, use large soda bottles with screw tops and fill them right to the top. If you can then keep whites and rosés in the refrigerator, and reds in a cool place, so much the better.

The following selection of reds, whites, and rosés includes 50 well-made wines at various prices. A gallon is equivalent to five bottles of American wine, a little more than five bottles of imported wine. The cheapest of these wines comes to 70¢ a bottle, more than a dozen come to less than $1.25 a bottle. Wines available only in half-gallons (HG), or in other sizes smaller than a gallon, are so indicated, but their prices have been calculated by the gallon.

Red Wines

$3.50–$6	Franzia Burgundy
	Juan Hernandez Spanish Burgundy
	Gallo Burgundy
	Italian Swiss Colony Burgundy
	Winemaster's Guild Burgundy
	Gallo Hearty Burgundy
	CK Mondavi Burgundy
	AGE Rioja
$6–$8	Pagni Chianti
	Martini Mountain Red
	Latada Portuguese Red
	Ecu Royal Claret Reserve (HG)
	Soderi Chianti
	Paul Masson Burgundy (HG)
	Rusticano (68 oz.)
	Christian Brothers Claret
	Inglenook Vintage Zinfandel (HG)
	Korbel Mountain Red (HG)
$8–$12	Suali Chianti
	Ruffino Valpolicella
	Nathaniel Johnston Grand Chartrons (68 oz.)

Bolla Valpolicella
Bertani Valpolicella
Ruffino Chianti

White Wines

$3.50–$6   North Mountain Chablis
Italian Swiss Colony Haut Sauterne
Gallo Chablis Blanc
Italian Swiss Colony Napa-Sonoma-Mendocino Chablis
Cantina Sociale Marino (60 oz.)
Almadén Mountain White Chablis

$6–$8   Martini Mountain White
Paul Masson Chablis (HG) *and* Dry Sauterne (HG)
Ecu Royal Blanc de Blancs (HG)
Inglenook Navalle Rhine (51 oz.)
Gold Seal Chablis Nature (HG)
Christian Brothers Chablis *and* Sauterne
Rusticano (68 oz.)
Inglenook Vintage Chablis (HG)
Great Western Aurora Sauterne (HG)

Rosés

$3.50–$5   North Mountain Vin Rosé
Guild Tavola Rosé
Gallo Pink Chablis
Italian Swiss Colony Pink Chablis

$6–$8   Inglenook Navalle Rosé (51 oz.)
Almadén Mountain Nectar Vin Rosé
Taylor Lake Country Pink (HG)
Christian Brothers Napa Rosé
Widmer Lake Roselle (HG)

APPENDIX 3

Comparative Price Ranges of Inexpensive Wines

The wines below are grouped section by section in the same order as they appear in this book. The thin line indicates the over-all price range of each group of wines; the heavy line suggests the price range within which the best values are to be found, which is not always at the cheapest end of the scale. Each wine listed can be found in the Index.

Red Wines

FRANCE

Beaujolais
Bordeaux Rouge, Médoc, and St.-Emilion
Petits Châteaux of Bordeaux
Bourgogne Rouge and Pinot Noir
Bourgueil, Chinon, and Saumur-Champigny
Corbières, Minervois, and Fitou
Côtes-du-Rhône

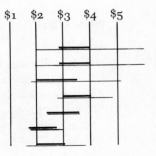

APPENDIXES

	$1	$2	$3	$4	$5

ITALY
Barbera
Chianti
Lambrusco
Valpolicella and Bardolino
Valtellina, Inferno, Grumello, and Sassella

SPAIN
Rioja

PORTUGAL
Dão

YUGOSLAVIA
Cabernet, Prokupac, and Plavac

HUNGARY
Egri Bikavér and Szeksárdi Vörös

GREECE
Red Wine

CHILE
Cabernet Sauvignon and Burgundy

UNITED STATES
California: Burgundy, Claret, and Chianti
California: Cabernet Sauvignon, Zinfandel,
    Gamay, and Gamay Beaujolais
New York State: Burgundy, Claret, and
    Red Wine

White Wines

FRANCE
Alsatian Riesling and Sylvaner
Bordeaux Blanc and Graves
Bourgogne Blanc, Mâcon Blanc, and
    Pinot Chardonnay
Muscadet
Sauternes and Barsac
Vouvray

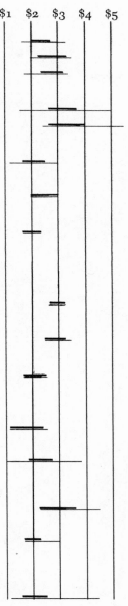

ITALY
  Frascati
  Orvieto
  Soave

GERMANY
  Rhine and Moselle: Regional Wines
  Single Vineyard Wines

SPAIN
  Rioja

PORTUGAL
  Vinho Verde

YUGOSLAVIA
  Šipon, Rizling, Traminec, and others

HUNGARY
  Debröi Hárslevelü, Badacsonyi
    Szürkebarát, and Csopaki
    Olasrizling

AUSTRIA
  Gumpoldskirchner

GREECE
  White Wines

UNITED STATES
  California: Chablis, Sauterne, and
    Rhine Wine
  California: Sweet Sauterne and
    Sweet Semillon
  California: Pinot Chardonnay, Chenin Blanc,
    Sauvignon Blanc, Johannisberg Riesling, and
    Riesling
  New York State: Chablis, Sauterne, and
    White Wine

Rosés

Rosés of the World

Index

Index

[Includes only those wine names in bold face type.]

INDEX

156

ACKNOWLEDGMENTS

Although all of the selections in *Guide to Inexpensive Wines* are
my own, a number of people joined me for one or another of the
many tastings I arranged for this book. I was delighted to have
their company and would like to express my thanks to those who
stopped by on several occasions: Arthur Amster, Gerald Asher,
William Clifford, David and Margaret Dorsen, Tim Enos, Roberto
Ferin, Ann Geracimos, Robert Haas, Fred Halliday, Perry Kozlow,
Charles Mueller, William Olcott, Dominique Rickard, Cliff
Roberson, Peter M. F. Sichel, Lucio Sorré, and Paul and Ann
Sperry. I would also like to thank Robert Lescher for consistently
maintaining a polite interest in inexpensive wines, while drinking
my Pétrus and my Richebourg.